Warp & Weft

WOVEN TEXTILES IN FASHION, ART AND INTERIORS

Warp & Weft

WOVEN TEXTILES IN FASHION, ART AND INTERIORS

Jessica Hemmings

BLOOMSBURY

LONDON · BERLIN · NEW YORK · SYDNEY

First published in Great Britain 2012
Bloomsbury Publishing Plc
50 Bedford Square
London WC1B 3DP
www.bloomsbury.com

ISBN: 978-1-4081-3444-3

A CIP catalogue record for this book is available from the
British Library

Publisher: Susan James
Managing editor: Davida Saunders
Page designer: Susan McIntyre
Cover designer: Sutchinda Thompson
Copy editor: Fiona Corbridge
Proofreader: Jane Anson

This book is produced using paper that is made from wood
grown in managed, sustainable forests. It is natural, renewable and
recyclable. The logging and manufacturing processes conform to
the environmental regulations of the country of origin.

Printed and bound in China

COVER IMAGE: Anne Wilson, *Wind-Up: Walking the Warp*, 2008. Performance and sculpture. First performed at the Rhona Hoffman Gallery, Chicago, USA, 20–25 January 2008. Participants included Carla Duarte, Annie Egleson, Surabhi Ghosh, Jongock Kim, Rosemary Lee, Christy Matson, Rachel Moore, Jeroen Nelemans, Sara Rabinowitz, Rana Siegel, Mike Slattery and Anne Wilson. PHOTOGRAPHER: SURABHI GHOSH. IMAGE COURTESY OF THE ARTIST AND RHONA HOFFMAN GALLERY, CHICAGO

FRONTISPIECE: Ball-Nogues Studio, *Gravity's Loom* (detail), 2010. Ink-dyed nylon twine installation, Indianapolis Museum of Art, USA. PHOTOGRAPHER: HADLEY FRUITS. IMAGE COURTESY OF THE INDIANAPOLIS MUSEUM OF ART

Contents

INTRODUCTION   7

CHAPTER ONE   THREADS   11

CHAPTER TWO   LIGHT   28

CHAPTER THREE   MOTION   51

CHAPTER FOUR   SOUND   70

CHAPTER FIVE   EMOTION   88

CHAPTER SIX   COMMUNITY   104

NOTES   133

FURTHER READING   141

INDEX   143

Introduction

THE INTENTION OF THIS BOOK IS TO REVEAL THE VAST RANGE of interdisciplinary connections that inspire and inspiration that informs recent woven textile art and design. While weaving is, in many ways, technical, content here is organised thematically into sections that I hope readers will find both familiar and, at times – such as the wealth of projects that explore weaving and sound – unexpected. A number of recurring areas of investigation appear across the thematic chapters. The binary system that underpins the weave structure and its relationship to our digital communication age is a rich area of inquiry. The pros and cons of hand and industrial production are apparent throughout, often with designers moving back and forth between the two in an increasing acceptance of the potential of digital tools coupled with acknowledgement of the vital importance of the weaver's hand. The tools of weaving are also a point of debate, from the adaptation of existing tools to the adoption of equipment from other disciplines, and even the invention of new tools to aid design and production. The impact new materials have on woven textile innovation is a further area of inquiry.

Weaving faces the curious challenge of besting the remarkable technical feats of previous centuries. It is something of a legacy and a burden. If we pause to look back, the celebrated weaver and educator Anni Albers, writing in 1946, noted:

It is easy to visualize how intrigued, as much as mystified, a weaver of ancient Peru would be in looking over the textiles of our day. Having been exposed to the greatest culture in the history of textiles and having been himself a contributor to it, he can be considered a fair judge of our achievements. He would marvel, we can imagine, at the speed of mass production, at the uniformity of threads, the accuracy of weaving and the low price. He would enjoy the new yarns used ... But strangely enough, he may find that neither one would serve him in his specific interest: the intricate interlocking of two sets of threads at right angles – weaving.[1]

OPPOSITE: Astrid Krogh, *Ikat I*, 2011. Fibre optic and paper weft and paper warp, plain weave hand-woven on ARM loom, 250 x 150 cm (99 x 59 in.).

PHOTOGRAPHER: TORBEN ESKEROD

LEFT: Aleksandra Gaca, *Tero* (detail), 2011, from Architextile collection. Cotton, wool, viscose, polyester and paper weft and cotton warp, various weave structures, Jacquard loom.

PHOTOGRAPHER: ALEKSANDRA GACA

RIGHT: Sarah Taylor, *Inner Light: Programmable Stripes*, material 2009, light design 2011. Polymer optical fibre weft activated by the use of LEDs, nylon monofilament warp, weft-faced weave structure hand-woven on Dobby loom with micro-controllers using a digital interface (DMX system), 15 x 40 cm (6 x 15¾ in.).

PHOTOGRAPHER: SARAH TAYLOR

The artists and designers selected for this book all embrace an expansive view of weaving. Some take the woven structure into new territory through their use of innovative materials, as Albers noted over half a century ago. Others challenge expected applications of the woven textile and introduce the structure to unfamiliar or unexpected settings. Still others draw heavily on interdisciplinary collaborations to invite new input to the purpose and potential of the woven textile.

Over the course of writing this book I have heard again and again of the weaver's sensibility, a way of approaching the visual and material world that guides thinking far beyond the construction of cloth. Arthur Danto has observed that 'the industrialization of the weaving process has set between most of us and the reality of weaving a cognitive barrier'.[2] He refers to this 'barrier' as 'opaque enough that it must come as a surprise that Plato should have found common to the arts of weaving and of statesmanship a quality of mind that is very central to the practice of an art, namely a certain kind of creative judgement – the ability to make decisions in the absence of rules or of laws'.[3] I understand the weaver's vision to be just this, an ability to work within the discipline and logic of weaving, while remaining alert to serendipity and trusting creative intuition.

In September of 2010 I organised a one-day symposium about inter-disciplinary approaches to weaving. The event was planned to coincide with a series of exhibitions supported by the Laura Ashley Foundation and curated by Laura Thomas for the Oriel Myrddin Gallery in Wales. Enthusiasm, and perhaps more tellingly, hunger for dialogue about woven textiles during

Salt, *Alternate Longitude* (detail), 2009. Stainless-steel weft and cotton and viscose warp, hand-woven on a Dobby loom.

PHOTOGRAPHER: MATTHEW JUDD

this event, prompted my work on this book. The title – *Warp and Weft* – is inherited from Laura Thomas's exhibition at the Oriel Myrddin Gallery. A number of individuals have been incredibly generous in their suggestions for artists and designers to consider for this book, in particular Philippa Brock, Anne Marie Commandeur, Lia Cook, Petter Hellsing, Beatrijs Sterk, Laura Thomas, Jereon Vinken and Anne Wilson. My sincere thanks to Dawn Youll and Cove Park, Scotland for an invaluable Creative Catalyst Residency funded by the Jerwood Foundation during August of 2011. My final thanks are reserved for the Rhode Island School of Design, where I spent four very happy years learning to weave as an undergraduate student. In the final event I did not become a weaver, but I am convinced that my time at the loom taught me how to write.

CHAPTER ONE

Threads

It is not uncommon for weavers to cite the creation of 'something out of nothing' as one of the wonders of weaving. But long before cloth exists, there are individual threads and a number of artists and designers make these threads the focus of their work. Working with thread brings its own unique challenges. How do you keep it in place? In fact, in the case of large-scale installations, how do you even get it in place? Examples discussed in this chapter are made by artists who choose to work alone, preferring control over efficiency, as well as those who work with teams, either of studio assistants or volunteers. Some invite mistakes into their working process, while others plan for perfection. All have had to develop their own systems to map and plan the execution of work that often does not want to stay put. In many cases, it is human hands that wind countless threads back and forth in what have to be admired as feats of great patience. For others, purpose-built tools are imagined and constructed to aid in the creation process. Nothing more than a quick snip from a pair of scissors de-installs some of these works, but not before viewers have been shown how the most modest of materials can make us reconsider the foundation of woven cloth.

'Take one step and it all changes' warns Mexican artist **Gabriel Dawe** of the installations he makes from coloured polyester thread.[1] Thousands of threads, hooked around nails and held under tension, make up each of his optically illusive works. In early versions of the 'Plexus' series, this meant Dawe was 'climbing up and down a ladder three hundred times a day' to wind threads back and forth. It was an installation technique he concedes was 'hard on the knees!' and, over time, his production strategies have slowly gained efficiency. Dawe trained as a graphic designer and absorbed 'the mindset that you have to produce commercial work. And if you want to be an artist, you have to sell "something" '. 'I was torn. My work with thread takes so long [to create]. It is not practical'. After a decade's work as a graphic designer left him decidedly burnt out, he returned to education as a postgraduate student at the University of Texas at Dallas. The experience 'got rid of the mindset that I have to produce to sell'.

Prior to working with thread, Dawe explored embroidery and paint. 'I used embroidery out of my childhood frustration. I grew up in a macho culture –

OPPOSITE: Gabriel Dawe, *Plexus 3*, 2010. Polyester thread installation, 3.65 x 1.82 x 4.88 m (12 x 6 x 16 ft), installed Guerilla Arts, USA.

PHOTOGRAPHER: KEVIN TODORA

Gabriel Dawe, *Plexus 4*, 2010. Polyester thread installation, 3.35 x 7.62 x 7.62 m (11 x 25 x 25 ft), installed Dallas Contemporary, USA.

PHOTOGRAPHER: KEVIN TODORA

Mexico – and in the summers my grandmother taught my sister embroidery. I was not taught because I was a boy. It was so frustrating. I didn't dare ask, but I remember trying to steal thread to do it.' Today he has come to terms with his chosen materials and the hours their installation demands. Projects range from work that is planned prior to installation with a space in mind, to work Dawe refers to as more 'generic' in its relationship to site, often as part of group exhibitions.

Working on-site with such a vast volume of thread comes with its risks. Remarkably, with the exception of some recent large commissions, he tends to install work alone. 'I have to come to terms with mistakes', Dawe admits. 'Mistakes make it human and in a way I welcome them – just not too much! I do try to correct mistakes when I see them, but sometimes it is too late.' Recent projects have enjoyed a second life after the installations are taken down. Threads are disengaged from their nails or hooks, allowed to knot, and placed in a perspex box. 'I see them as relics of the piece', Dawe explains of these colourful tangles of what were once precisely ordered threads.

Gabriel Dawe *Plexus No. 2*, 2011. Polyester thread and plexiglass box from installation at Dallas Contemporary, USA, 21.6 x 21.6 x 22.9 cm (8½ x 8½ x 9 in.).

PHOTOGRAPHER: GARY STRUNK

Gabriel Dawe, *Plexus 5* (detail), 2011. Polyester thread installation, installed Pump Projects, Texas Biennial, USA.

PHOTOGRAPHER: MIKE METCALFE

Dawe's 'Plexus' series uses thread stretched taut and held under tension. In contrast, *Gravity's Loom*, by the Los Angeles-based **Ball-Nogues Studio**, works, as the name suggests, with gravity. Led by Benjamin Ball and Gaston Nogues, the studio's 'Suspension' series uses a range of materials in ceiling-mounted installations. *Gravity's Loom* was exhibited in the Indianapolis Museum of Art during late 2010 and early 2011 and was comprised of 1,900 pieces of cut twine in varying lengths. Each piece of twine was offset by 2 m (6 ft 6¾in.) and crossed another as they span the oval perimeter of one of the museum's entrance areas. The installation created a twisted and inverted dome shape, which Douglas Murphy observes as having 'porous spatial effects' that change as the viewer moves through the space.[2] Ball and Nogues, who both trained as architects, explain that the vibrant colours and patterns of the installation are inspired by the surface decoration of baroque domes that 'blur the distinction between what is architectural, sculptural, and pictorial'. 'The [painted] strings … represent the imagined plan for a traditional baroque ceiling pattern – a three-dimensional volume that will blur into billows of color and then snap into a focused geometry, depending on the viewer's vantage point.'[3]

LEFT, RIGHT AND BELOW:
Ball-Nogues Studio,
Gravity's Loom, 2010.
Ink-dyed nylon twine
installation, Indianapolis
Museum of Art, USA.
PHOTOGRAPHER: HADLEY FRUITS
IMAGES COURTESY OF THE INDIANAPOLIS
MUSEUM OF ART

Susie MacMurray,
Promenade, 2010.
Cotton thread installation,
Kedleston Hall, Derby,
England.

PHOTOGRAPHER: SUSIE MACMURRAY

A team of studio assistants work to cut and colour each piece of twine using the *Insta-llator 1 with the Variable Information Atomising Module* machine. The device was invented and fabricated by the pair to aid in the design process, as well as coordinate the measurement, cutting and airbrushing of each string into 'one continuous sequence of procedures that would be extremely time-consuming and tedious (impossible) for a human to accomplish'.[4] The 'machine eliminated the mind-boggling process of cutting by hand … individual lengths of string, no two alike … allowing us to precisely airbrush each string in discrete locations based on data input from a computer'.[5] The vibrant colours of the work can be likened to ikat textiles, a system of space-dyeing the weft and/or warp yarn prior to weaving to create predetermined patterns. On reflection, Ball describes the structure of *Gravity's Loom* as 'something akin to weaving, albeit not tightly woven'. 'We don't set out to reference weaving', he emphasises, although 'Weaving is a fundamental way of ordering matter'.[6]

British artist **Susie MacMurray** shares with Ball-Nogues Studio the fact that she 'was not thinking about weaving' when she responded to a commission by the National Trust to create an installation for Kedleston Hall, England in 2010.[7] But much like Ball-Nogues, a warp of kinds is the result. MacMurray

LEFT AND BELOW: Susie MacMurray, *Promenade*, 2010. Cotton thread installation, Kedleston Hall, Derby, England.

PHOTOGRAPHER: SUSIE MACMURRAY

PHOTOGRAPHER: MATTHEW ANDREWS

PHOTOGRAPHER: JULIAN HUGHES

worked to a project brief that asked specifically for an installation that spoke to visitors about the original purpose of the house. Her response was to amplify the owner's original intentions for the property. Kedleston Hall was inherited by Sir Nathaniel Curzon in 1758, who immediately knocked down the original building and began anew. The resulting Hall, designed by the architect Robert Adam, was intended to be a place where, in MacMurray's words 'you go to see and to be seen. It is about looking'.

Even when first built, the public were allowed to visit the Hall and admire the contents. In fact, the area where MacMurray installed her work was never lived in as a home and was always intended for the public gaze. With the busy foot traffic of curious National Trust visitors in mind, MacMurray constructed a work to highlight this original performance of looking. Over two weeks, several dozen volunteers helped to wind the 167 km (103¾ miles) of gold cotton 'warp' around the alabaster pillars of Kedleston's Marble Hall. The pillars essentially acted as a giant warping board. Cotton was chosen in case polyester thread proved tougher than the soft alabaster pillars; the colour was a response to an elaborate dress of woven gold thread once owned by the Curzon family. But rather than creating cloth, the work is first and foremost about directing vision.

The thread creates channels in space that are optically illusive, but also very real barriers and pathways that control each viewer's movement. 'I wanted visitors to be more intensely aware of their surroundings', MacMurray explains. Similar to the work of Dawe and Ball-Nogues Studio, the visibility of these routes is largely dependent on the vantage point of the viewer. Here the result encouraged a sense of scrutiny within the space, which highlighted the original preening and parading that was once the purpose of the site. Reflecting on this history, MacMurray explains, 'History is intangible, it never stops, you can never pin it down, never say *this is how it is.*' The shifting perspectives made material through the simple winding of thread help act as a reminder of this truth.

While Dawe and MacMurray stretch threads under tension and Ball-Nogues Studio allows gravity to determine shape, Welsh artist and designer **Laura Thomas** casts unwoven threads in resin. Resin eliminates the need for tension or gravity to hold the thread in place, instead allowing threads to float in space. Thomas trained as a weaver and these works are informed by her fascination with the potential, and limitations, of the woven structure. She refers to the work as a 'celebration of unwoven threads', but more recently wanted to return to the tactile qualities of weaving.[8] A residency at the Ruthin Craft Centre in Wales from 2009–11 allowed time for Thomas to engage in a making strategy that would otherwise have easily been deemed too time-intensive for her typical commercial work. Six solid weeks of weaving time on a dense warp of 60 ends per inch generated 80 m (87½ yd) of warp-faced plain weave. The fabric was then cut and re-woven by hand in a triaxial structure to create *Three*

Laura Thomas, *Three x Five*, (detail right), 2010. Triaxial hand weaving of woven strips of warp-faced plain weave, cotton, silk and linen 130 x 100 cm (51 x 39½ in.).

PHOTOGRAPHER: DEWI TANNATT LLOYD

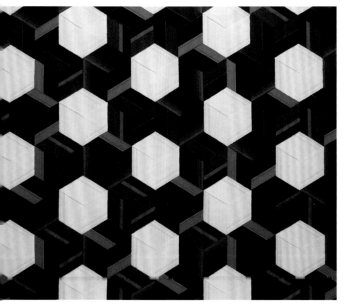

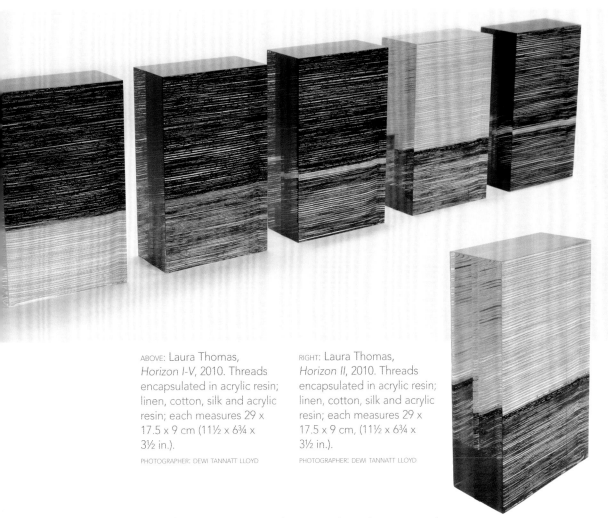

ABOVE: Laura Thomas, *Horizon I-V*, 2010. Threads encapsulated in acrylic resin; linen, cotton, silk and acrylic resin; each measures 29 x 17.5 x 9 cm (11½ x 6¾ x 3½ in.).

PHOTOGRAPHER: DEWI TANNATT LLOYD

RIGHT: Laura Thomas, *Horizon II*, 2010. Threads encapsulated in acrylic resin; linen, cotton, silk and acrylic resin; each measures 29 x 17.5 x 9 cm, (11½ x 6¾ x 3½ in.).

PHOTOGRAPHER: DEWI TANNATT LLOYD

x Five. Triaxial weaving, as the name suggests, does not place the warp and weft at right angles, but instead interweaves in three directions. The technique allowed Thomas to 'subvert the rules of cloth and the horizontal and vertical of warp and weft'.

The palette of *Three x Five* is 'loosely inspired by Welsh landscape colours' and the hand interweaving of the woven strips ordered only the yellow strips, leaving the remaining dark background to be random in what Thomas describes as 'ordered disorder'. Each of the woven strips that becomes the warp and weft of the finished work uses a strié effect of irregularly ordered different coloured threads. Yellow moves from mustard to near white, a black band gradually builds to forest green, a mottled blue turns to purple-black with a strip of brighter blue separating the two and brown sits besides purple, separated by one fine pick of coral. The result is an intricate weaving within a weaving that both respects and questions the logic of the woven structure.

British artist **Sue Lawty** is celebrated for her work as a tapestry weaver. But in recent years, materials such as stones and lead have found an increasingly prominent place in her work. 'I need to *not* know what I am doing', Lawty explains of her desire to continually challenge established ways of working.[9] 'It is not that I actively seek to do this, but I know that I am drawn to asking questions constantly.' In 2004, a chance encounter with a fellow artist working with lead showed Lawty 'the most beautiful pure line' and she instinctively recognised that the line 'wasn't thread, it was metal – lead – with a plumb bob on the bottom. This made the quality of that line in space so different'.

Lawty's work and the preliminary research that inspires it often have strong connections with the land, 'specifically with rock and increasingly with geology', she observes. 'The direct association of taking stuff from deep under the ground and weaving with it has an immediacy that is very exciting', she explains. 'I love the fact that lead is almost rock, but also soft, ductile, malleable – you can beat it with a hammer.' But for all these connections, lead hardly lends itself to weaving. Recalling her early samples, she concedes, 'Lead is awkward. It is not that pleasant to work with. It's when you start to feel the weight and the character of the lead fabric that things get interesting. The real thrill and control comes in the hammering process – sensing how much pressure [to apply] and when to stop. A crude structure pressed flat immediately starts to transform, to look like it has always been there.'

This 'been there' quality has long captured Lawty's eye. As artist in residence at the Victoria and Albert Museum in London during 2005–6, she noticed herself 'going back to the basics of cloth: plain-weave fabric. The things [in the V&A archive] I was drawn to most were simple little fragments and humble interlacement … hand-spun linens from Egypt; rhythmic marks from the hand of the maker and nuances of thread'. Lawty continues, 'I've always been fascinated by the way artefacts in museums are imbued with a sense of time – the strong visual metre of their construction worn and fragmented over the years. With the lead, the repetitive pattern of the structure is obvious, but through beating becomes indistinct and homogenous.'

Lawty explains, 'I have always been interested in the intrinsic visual language that emerges from working with the specific qualities of a material and structure. There is something about the unfinished, the broken-up, that is intriguing.' She cites the American poet Louise Glück, who writes, 'The unsaid, for me, exerts great power: often I wish an entire poem could be made in this vocabulary. It is analogous to the unseen for example, to the power of ruins, to works of art either damaged or incomplete. Such works inevitably allude to larger contexts; they haunt because they are not whole, though wholeness is implied: another time, a world in which they were whole, or were to have been whole, is implied. There is no moment in which their first home is felt to

Sue Lawty, *Lead Weave 1* (detail), 2006. Lead warp and weft, hand interlacing.

PHOTOGRAPHER: PETER KELLEHER

COURTESY OF V&A IMAGES, VICTORIA AND ALBERT MUSEUM, LONDON

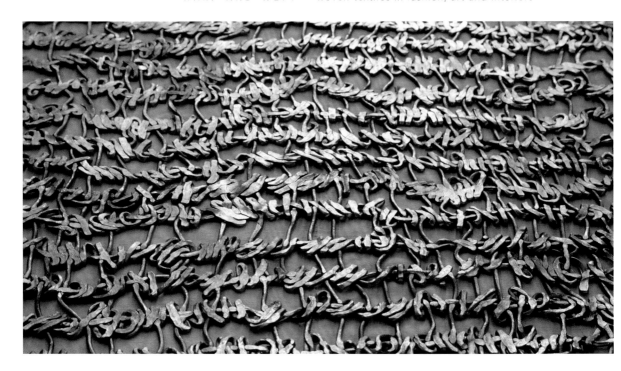

Sue Lawty, *Lead Weave* (detail), 2008. Lead warp and weft, vertical tapestry loom.

PHOTOGRAPHER: JERRY HARDMAN-JONES

be the museum.'[10] Reflecting on her own work, Lawty concludes, 'I really like honesty. I work with few materials and techniques. Weaving is such a fantastic, basic structure. I don't have preconceived notions of what I am going to do. The ambiguity of a corrupted structure is a real link with time, but there is a tension here between the stable longevity of lead and the vulnerable qualities of the woven fabric.'

Lawty builds up dimension when weaving lead and then beats the material away, constructing and then breaking down structure. Working with vastly different materials, British product designer **Lauren Moriarty** takes the structure of the woven textile and reduces three dimensions back into two dimensions in a different design cycle of deconstruction and reconstruction. In early work, Moriarty often took line drawings and close-up images of woven or stitched textiles as her starting point. These drawings were then scanned and overlaid in CAD to create new three-dimensional objects. In her more recent explorations, this design process has become more complex. Her deconstruction of existing woven structures and reconstruction of new repeating patterns continues to use the woven structure as the foundation. But she now uses a variety of combined processes from plotter-cut pieces (for cutting vector drawings) to laser-cutting and hand-cutting to make the woven structure material again.

OPPOSITE: Lauren Moriarty, *Stitch Studies No. 1* (detail), 2010. Laser-cut plastics.

PHOTOGRAPHER: ROB WARREN

'What I am interested in is an open-weave structure with holes and gaps in between', she explains of her ideal inspiration textile. Layers are then created, often taking several copies of one structure and exploring the

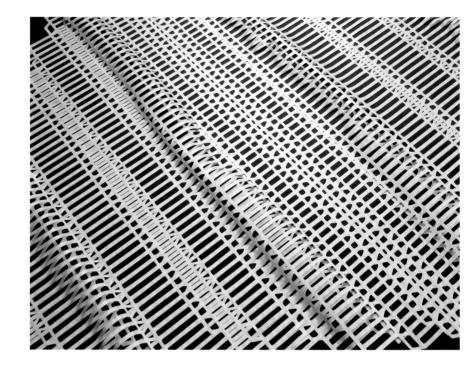

Lauren Moriarty, *Stitch Studies No. 6* (detail), 2011. Laser-cut plastics.

PHOTOGRAPHER: ROB WARREN

effects of offsetting and overlaying. Her current experiments are modest in size and more intricate than photographs might suggest. Even when digital tools are used as the first step in the process, hand finishing often completes the final work. 'There is no other way. If there was, I would explore it!' she exclaims.[11] In this recent experimental work, Moriarty has noticed that the balance between the contribution made by machine and what can be made by hand is 'a different way for me to work. Textile and product designers are always designing for *something*'. While the Ball–Nogues Studio looks to the machine to assist in the design process and then expedite a hand process with precision, Moriarty's experimental projects work closely with digital tools in the development of her designs, but benefit from hand finishing. Despite being undeniably labour–intensive, she welcomes the deviations that the hand brings. Each piece 'comes out a different way', she observes, in contrast to CAD, which 'always gives one outcome'. Essentially, hand finishing allows for the moment when happy accidents emerge. It is these slips and deviations that provide inspiration for the next step to be fed back into her tools.

Like Moriarty, American artist **Elana Herzog** does not weave cloth. Instead, she deconstructs woven cloth. Herzog attaches textiles to the walls of her installation sites with industrial staples and then pulls these fabrics from their new foundations, allowing a random pattern of cloth to remain. She explains: 'The late 1990s saw a gradual withering away of any independent structure in my pieces, until finally they became completely dependent upon their surroundings for support. I began working directly on the walls, embedding materials in drywall by channelling into it with screwdrivers and hammers, and by stapling fabric to its surface. Suddenly I was drawing, and the wall was an integral part of my pieces.'[12]

What remains is largely the result of chance: fabric at its strongest points overlaid with a new 'weave' of metal staples that create an under-and-over weave of their own. In a departure from previous works, *Plaid*, made in 2007, was the first instance when Herzog worked with fabric from a bolt rather than from existing textiles, such as the chenille bedspreads that were the basis of a number of previous works. The bolt of cloth used in *Plaid* was bought at the closing sale of a fabric shop, the last sale indicative (it is difficult not to make the leap in associations) of a worldwide shift in textile manufacturing centres. Along with this unplanned commentary, working with fabric from a bolt provided Herzog with the opportunity to leave the rectangular frame of the bedspread and its formal associations with painting and instead use the textile across an entire interior space. For the installation of *Plaid* at the Smack Mellon Gallery in Brooklyn, Herzog fabricated a pillar and low walls that she terms 'quasi-architectural forms' and sees as suggestive of an office environment.

Elana Herzog, *Plaid* (detail), 2007. Fabric and industrial staples, installation view at Smack Mellon Gallery, Brooklyn, USA.
PHOTOGRAPHER: ETIENNE FROSSARD

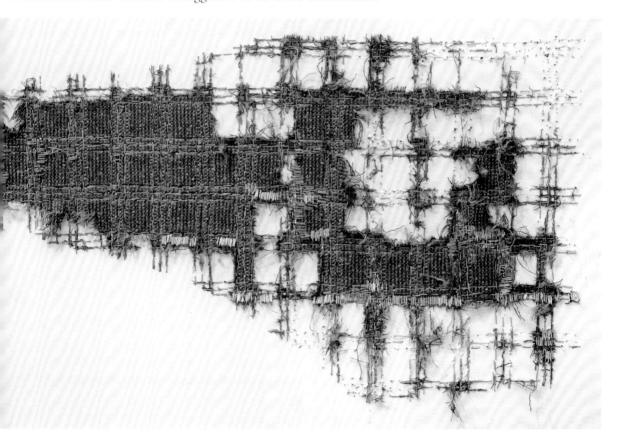

Textiles became a part of Herzog's visual vocabulary in 1989 and took up 'almost exclusive prominence a few years later'; stapled textiles emerged as a strategy in 1999. 'I like the woven structure partly because of its relationship to the grid', she explains. The fabric she chooses to work with tends to have an obvious weave. 'When I became interested in the conspicuous weave [of certain textiles] it was partly because I was able to generate an image with staples that had both vertical and horizontal elements that overlapped – a different kind of drawing builds up. In some part of my mind I am using staples to reconstruct something that is woven – so the form is being generated and not just in a linear drawing way.' In an interview with Regine Basha, Herzog explains, 'The staple is, in fact, analogous to a stitch or a suture, so in some way I am re-imagining the structure of a textile and dramatizing its production. I often think of my pieces as replacing the existing binary language of warp and weft with a corresponding binary system whose two elements are metal staples and fabric.'[13]

Like many of the examples in this chapter, Herzog expresses uneasiness with the idea that the textile should offer the primary interpretation of her work. Instead, she situates her work within the history of fine art, while acknowledging her discomfort with many of the categories of identification this provides. '*Plaid* aspires to both austerity and excess. It is simultaneously garish and restrained. It has a relationship to modernism, both reverent and irreverent, as does much of my work. This is the language I grew up with, but have never felt ownership of. To the extent that I operate from a position of alienation, my relationship to both high and low culture remains vicarious. I've always thought of myself as a sculptor, and enjoy tinkering with that identity. My materials, often cheap, tacky, or discarded household items and fabric, challenge conventions of taste and beauty and draw attention to how art and design migrate throughout culture, from high to low and back again, reinterpreted by industry to meet the needs of different markets and trends … I am fascinated by the way form is generated by growth and decay, construction and destruction.'[14]

Elana Herzog, *Plaid*, 2007.
Fabric and industrial staples,
installation view at Smack
Mellon Gallery, Brooklyn,
USA.

PHOTOGRAPHER: ETIENNE FROSSARD

CHAPTER TWO

Light

TEXTILES THAT CAPTURE AND REFLECT LIGHT range from the low-tech to the high-tech and often present shifting qualities as our physical location changes the way that we observe them. Shiny materials such as lurex and yarns woven with tiny reflective glass beads encourage light to bounce off their surfaces. At the other end of the technical spectrum, fibre optics channel light from a source through their core. Woven textiles also filter and disrupt light to cast beautiful shadows. Changes in natural light over the course of the day, as well as artificial light powered by electricity and programmed to shift colour and intensity, mean the surfaces of textiles that play with light are ever-changing.

Dutch artist and designer **Tamar Frank** creates large-scale permanent installations that often use LED lights. In 2006, working with the Galerie Het Langhuis in Zwolle, the Netherlands, she 'wove' monofilament from the floor to the ceiling of a second-floor attic in the gallery's 17th-century building. '[The] whole construction of the building foundation is sunken on one side,' Frank explains, 'and the attic floor is at such an angle that your first sensation is you are falling and have to compensate with your balance.'[1] Frank responded to the somewhat precarious angle of the floor by 'making the opposite angle with threads – an image that the threads are holding up the floor'. Nylon monofilament, more commonly used as fishing line, created the ethereal structure-within-a-structure. When viewed in natural light, the monofilament provides an illusive demarcation in the space that looks, at times, like beams of natural light. From other perspectives, the lines disappear completely. For the exhibition, which took place during winter's short days, Frank blacked out what was left of the natural light and added hidden UV tube lighting to illuminate the monofilament line.

Frank describes installing the work as 'almost like weaving. I made connections with a staple gun in advance and looped ten threads at a time'. While her practice more typically creates permanent installations, this installation was temporary. The visual fragility of the work is deceptive: monofilament can bear a surprising weight. In fact, Frank's only major concern at the opening was that cigarette embers might melt through the

Tamar Frank, *Light Installation 1 and 2*, 2006. Nylon monofilament installation seen: (above left) in natural light; (above right) with UV tube lighting (detail, right), Galerie Het Langhuis in Zwolle, the Netherlands.

PHOTOGRAPHER: TAMAR FRANK

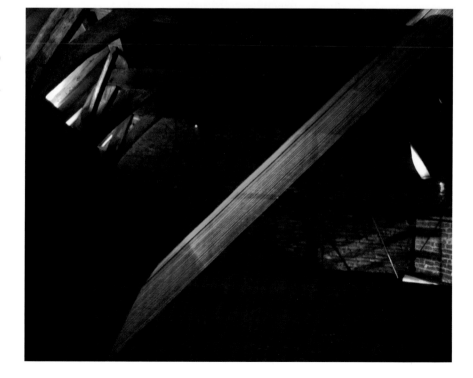

strands. 'I work with light, but I am getting approached more from a textile perspective because I am working with threads', she observes. 'If you think of where the textile comes from, it begins with the one thread. This is almost like taking the textile back to its source.'

Fellow Dutch designer **Marianne Kemp** explains that she is 'not interested in weaving patterns, but in texture'.[2] As a student at the Royal Academy of Art in The Hague, Kemp considered how to 'bring the outside inside'. Her initial response to the idea used plant fibres and today she continues to work only with natural fibres. Her trademark is horsehair – a material that is naturally flame retardant and stronger than leather. 'One [horse] tail in one colour will in fact have many colours that give a nuanced effect when used in lighting', she explains. The fibre's natural rigidity also provides volume. *Ray Light* is constructed as a flexible weft-faced tube on the loom. The horsehair weft and linen warp provide volume and maintain the tube structure.

Collaborations with designers from fields such as fashion and product design help introduce Kemp to new ways of working. Her collaborators tend to 'look at my material in a different way', she observes. *Ray Light* was made in collaboration with the interior architect Karel Bodegom, who invited Kemp to design lighting to exhibit in his showroom in Bas van Pelt, The Hague. Bodegom designed the adaptable hanging system for the light, leaving Kemp to do what she enjoys most: weaving. 'It is good to collaborate with others who have knowledge of different materials and techniques,' she explains, 'as this helps to make a strong object.'

The British company **Dashing Tweeds**, led by Kirsty McDougall and Guy Hills, is on a quest to reinvigorate traditional tweed weaving. Working to integrate new technology and traditional production, the company is committed to updating tweed, a woven cloth commonly associated with Scottish heritage. Hills – a photographer and avid cyclist – and McDougall, who trained as a weaver, hit upon the idea soon after meeting in 2003. McDougall explains: 'I remember when we first met we talked about photography processes and light effects and how we might combine his interest in light and my interest in functional tweed textiles.'[3]

McDougall states that 'Tweed was made as the original material for sportswear, but Dashing Tweeds updates this provenance for the growing cycling market in urban areas.'[4] Trademarked Lumatwill™ in 2005, their fabric contains a reflective filament yarn made of glass beads manufactured by 3M (the same as used on the back of builders' jackets) and a worsted or tweed wool yarn. What initially looks to be traditional suiting becomes reflective in certain lights. McDougall explains: 'Dashing Tweeds appeals to a menswear market that doesn't want an obviously innovative-looking aesthetic but enjoys the technical aspect through hidden innovation in a heritage-inspired textile.'[5]

OPPOSITE AND ABOVE: Marianne Kemp, *Ray Light* (details), 2011. Horsehair weft and linen warp with fluorescent tube, weft-faced plain weave, Lervad loom.

PHOTOGRAPHER: ROGIER CHANG

Dashing Tweeds, 'Block'
collection, 2009. Merino
wool and reflective yarn weft
and merino wool warp, satin
and sateen block structure
hand-woven on ARM loom.

PHOTOGRAPHER: GUY HILLS

Dashing Tweeds, 'Raver'
collection, 2009. Merino
wool and reflective yarn
weft and merino wool
warp, variable twill structure
hand-woven on ARM loom.

PHOTOGRAPHER: GUY HILLS

The company's first product, a reflective scooter coat, was developed as a response to requests and what the pair saw as a gap in the market. Enthusiasm from the cycling fraternity has now led them to expand the collection to include coats, a cycling cape and flat cap, all woven in the UK. McDougall observes, 'The development of intelligent textiles came with a certain aesthetic.' Rather than follow the slick, space age plastics popular at the turn of the millennium,

Dashing Tweeds, *Scooter Coat* (day view), 2007. Merino wool and reflective yarn weft and merino wool warp, twill structure.
PHOTOGRAPHER: GUY HILLS

Dashing Tweeds, *Scooter Coat* (night view), 2007. Merino wool and reflective yarn weft and merino wool warp, twill structure.
PHOTOGRAPHER: GUY HILLS

Dashing Tweeds uses 'ideas of heritage to hide the technical'. Tweed or worsted suiting is treated as 'a "carrier" for technical and functional yarns', essentially concealing its unexpected reflective properties within a traditional pattern. McDougall's daring eye for colour and commitment to the heritage of British weaving plays to the strengths of the durable cloth. By marketing it through the clever eye of a photographer, the pair are giving tweed a new lease of life.

Dashing Tweeds, *BT Tower*, 2009. Merino wool and reflective yarn weft and merino wool warp, satin and sateen block structure, suit tailored by Huntsman.

PHOTOGRAPHER: GUY HILLS

Japanese designer **Hiroko Takeda** describes her design aesthetic as 'expressing incongruous harmonies'.[6] From her studio in Brooklyn, New York, Takeda divides her time between commercial design for the high-end textile market and her own artistic practice. 'The world of industrial design can often be impersonal so, in my work as an independent designer, I also try to create an intimacy and sensitivity', she explains.[7] For example, Takeda wove by hand *Metal Flower*, a combination of linen and lurex, as an antidote to the manufacturing questions that occupy much of her time. The contrasting surfaces epitomise her interest in 'incongruous harmonies'. Expanding on her poetic list of aesthetic qualities, she elaborates: '[A] balance within an unbalanced space, an organic element arising from a synthetic structure … these lead me to experiment endlessly with materials and techniques.'[8]

Takeda states: 'I use metallic yarn at times to create a luminosity that contrasts with other materials in the fabric. When I use such luminous materials, I often construct a solid area, instead of using one or two threads as an accent. In *Metal Flower*, it creates a mirror effect, a shimmering light that contrasts and yet harmonises with the dry linen fibre in the fabric. It reminds me of the quality and effect of the autumn through winter light in Tokyo, where I grew up. The buildings and streets are grey and dry but the brilliant, clean light transforms the fabric of the city.'[9] 'The purpose of the textile doesn't matter!' Takeda defends, it is 'something to use or have as an artwork: I don't categorise'.

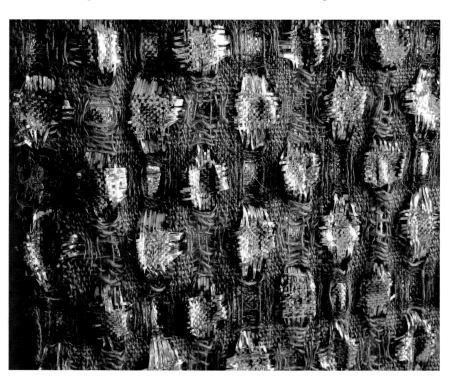

Hiroko Takeda, *Metal Flower* (detail), 2009. Linen and lurex, hand-woven on an AVL loom.

PHOTOGRAPHER: HIROKO TAKEDA

'Weaving something invisible' was the original challenge behind German artist **Christine Keller**'s 'Light Content: Points of View' series woven in 2004.[10] The seven Jacquard-woven panels were created at the Hexagram Institute of Concordia University and the Montreal Centre for Contemporary Textiles in Canada, using imagery Keller photographed in Montreal. She explains, 'I realised you could weave in layers that were only visible in certain lights. My idea was to make a grey fabric where you could only see the image in a certain light.' While the idea of hiding an image within a woven structure may sound simple enough, the technical realisation of the project proved an enormous challenge. 'It was a simple idea, but needed complex processing to weave', Keller remembers. The straightforward part of the idea comes from the nature of reflection itself: 'Reflective threads (also manufactured by 3M) have lots of mirrors like microscopic balls, and reflection bounces straight back to where light comes from. So you can only see the image if the light is directed at eye level on to the cloth and reflected back.' The less straightforward part of the project involved the drafting of two image layers and their interconnection as well as access to the specialist equipment needed to weave the project.

To expose the imagery in the work, the viewer holds a light to the weaving. The direction of light falling on the fabric's surface determines which imagery is visible. 'During the time I made this work, it was very fashionable to make everything "interactive" between man and technology, and I did not want sensors to go off as someone walked in', Keller says of her decision to invite viewers to manually direct a light at the work. 'It was important for me to let viewers have control over the light.'[11] The manual application of light by viewers confirms, for any doubting Thomas, that there are no engineering tricks behind the scenes to control the imagery. If you are standing beside someone holding a light, you may not see the same image as the person nearby, because the light will not bounce back in multiple directions. Natural daylight provides a similar effect over time. The angle of the light hitting the fabric determines where the image is visible.[12] As a result, the viewing experience, alluded to in the subtitle – *Points of View* – is entirely individual. Keller extends this reading beyond the textile, pointing out: 'This is happening in real life all the time. We think we talk about the same thing, at the same time, but everyone has their own perception.'

The woven imagery of the 'Light Content' series is based on photographs the artist shot in Montreal of steel structures once admired as cutting-edge engineering. 'There was a time when these were new technologies', Keller explains of the steel bridge arch. 'We think digital looms controlled by computer are modern and those bridges are now old museum pieces – we should not get too excited about fashions of technology.' Now based in New Zealand, Keller has faced challenges in accessing the looms required to develop the project further that have caused her to a reassess her interest in digital weaving. She

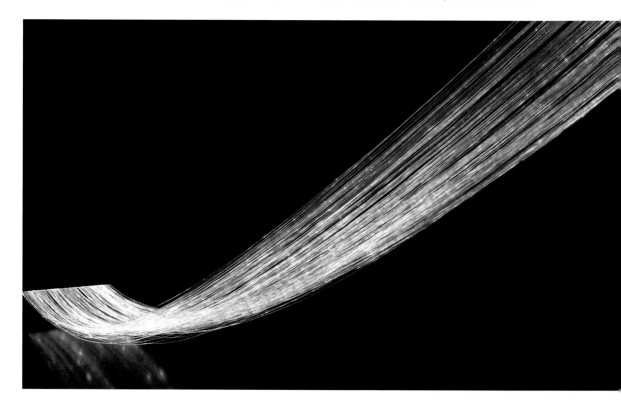

Hilde Hauan Johnsen and Maia Urstad, *01001*, 2007. Optic fibre and audio, 1 x 10 m (3 ft 4 in. x 32 ft 10 in.).

PHOTOGRAPHER: THOR BRØDRESKIFT

admits to her ongoing 'fascination with new technology' but has also found herself revisiting 'the potential of plain weave'. 'High technologies are fragile', she concludes, and 'it is dangerous to totally rely on them'.

Norwegian artist **Hilde Hauan Johnsen** describes installation *01001* as a 'sonic web using fibre optics'.[13] The work, made in collaboration with sound artist Maia Urstad, was created at the time Norway switched from an analogue to a national digital terrestrial TV and radio network in 2007, and is named after the binary number system. Hauan Johnsen points out that fibre optics are now the global medium for transmitting electronic signals and these 'invisible waves of voices and noise are constantly flowing through us without our being aware of anything other than the final result, i.e. when the mobile phone rings or websites appear on the computer screen'.[14] In *01001*, both ends of the optic fibres are connected to white light sources, which change in intensity via signals from an interface that translates sound into light depending on the frequency and amplitude, not simply the volume, of the audio component.

'Telecommunication activities serve as raw material for the sound composition, i.e. sounds recorded before and after passing through a broadband network, the tapping from a PC keyboard, telephone signals, voices, numbers, fragments of telephone conversations and interference/"ether noise", referring to the inaudible and invisible universe of signals soaring through the air at all

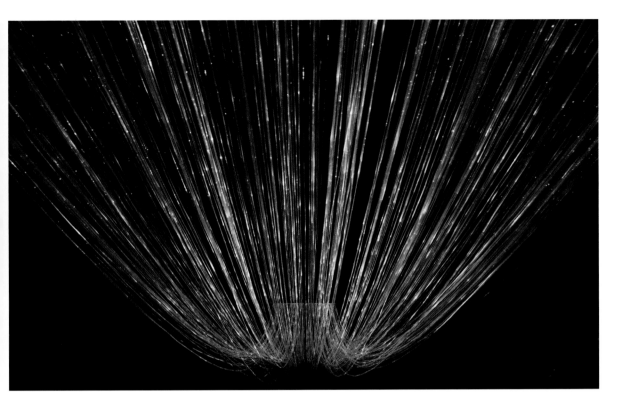

times',[15] Hauan Johnsen volunteers. 'When you are in the space you can hear white noise, but you don't know if it is a telephone or from outer space. The communication is "as if" all the broadband communication that uses fibre optics goes through these fibres.'[16]

The white light *01001* emits ranges from 'bright to almost bluish, pink and yellow according to the type of sound' and radiates from the end of the optic fibres as well as areas Hauan Johnsen has scoured with sandpaper and small cuts. The pulsating light provides a constant reminder of the communication traffic that now runs throughout each day. 'Even during moments of silence the fibres can be illuminated by transmitting a frequency below the speaker range, making the sound "visible" without hearing it.'[17] The work is held together in a bundle and 'stretched in a comb to keep them apart from each other with a thread woven to keep each [optic fibre] divided from another'. Ten metre-long versions of *01001* were displayed in 2007 at the 'Kaunas Art Biennial: Textiles' and in 2007–8 at the National Museum's Zilinskas Gallery in Lithuania. In late 2008, an extended version measuring 30 m (98 ft 6 in.) was exhibited at the Bryne Railway Station near Stavanger. 'Viewers sit for a long time,' Hauan Johnsen observes of the installation, 'mentally trying to figure it out. The sounds are beautiful – not ugly white noise – but noises you recognise as though you have been there.'

Hilde Hauan Johnsen and Maia Urstad, *01001* (detail), 2007. Optic fibre and audio.
PHOTOGRAPHER: THOR BRØDRESKIFT

Sarah Taylor, *Inner Light: Programmable Stripes*, 2009, Polymer optical fibre and optical fibre paper-based weft activated by the use of micro-crontrolled LEDs using a digital interface, DMX relplay system, nylon monofilament and paper warp, weft-faced weave structure hand-woven on Dobby loom, 15 x 40 cm (6 x 15¾ in.).

PHOTOGRAPHER: SARAH TAYLOR

British designer **Sarah Taylor** has worked with fibre optics since 1992 and investigates 'novel, time-based aesthetics within cloth'.[18] In recent samples, Taylor has developed a polymer optical fibre made from a non-woven, paper-based yarn housing a pre-treated optical fibre. While Hilde Hauan Johnsen treated the surface of her fibre optics with sandpaper and incisions, Taylor uses laser etching to allow light loss in predetermined locations and encases the optical fibre yarn in laminated paper. The etching creates pattern, while the paper enhances the light emission and provides a particular diffused light quality. Taylor reveals that the 'coloured light is the result of laser-etching the optical fibre to predetermine light loss as pattern in the yarn and is illuminated with pre-designed colour sequences controlled by a digital-mix DMX replay system'. In recent research the cloth is lit by tri–LEDs (red, green, blue), which allow the opportunity for sophisticated colour mixing. Circatron Limited developed the electronic mechanism to control the LEDs that light the optical fibre and the digital micro-controller.

Taylor goes on to say that 'As optical fibre does not emit UV light or transmit heat or electricity, it is suitable for use in both fashion and interiors. It is made from a thin glass or polymer core covered with cladding along which light travels without escaping.'[19] 'The encased light can be released by hand-weaving the polymer optical fibres. This was pioneered during my research degree at Heriot-Watt University (then, the Scottish College of Textiles), completed in 1995, and causes the fibres to abrade and allow light to escape through the cladding. The result is a visual sensation of colour and light.'[20] Taylor anticipates that application of this research can extend far beyond the decorative. 'What I am excited about is the properties this light source can

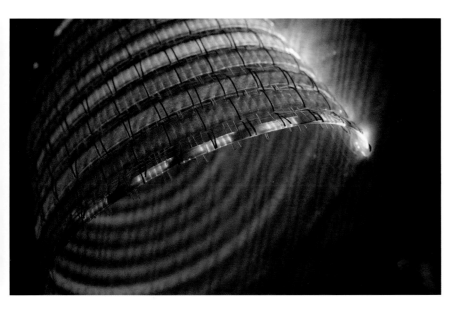

have within new markets that are product and well-being oriented. Given the importance the correct use of light can have on our well-being, this, to me, is the future development in lighting technology and design.'[21]

Danish designer **Astrid Krogh**'s 2011 series, 'Ikat I–III', is woven with optic fibres and paper yarn, programmed to emit a changing combination of colours. Krogh began to work with fibre optics in 2000 for the 'Lightmail' exhibition, based on the theme of curtains, at the Trapholt Museum in Kolding, Denmark. During the project she found her thinking shifted from using the textile to filter daylight to an interest in trying to weave with light itself. Two years later, an exhibition at the Museum for Decorative Arts in Copenhagen (now renamed Designmuseum Denmark) drew together inspiration from the museum's textile collection, in particular Gobelin tapestries, and her interest in weaving fibre optics. Today she states: 'I use light as both a material and a technology … Light enables my textiles to pulsate, change patterns and create an entire spectrum of ever-changing colourways.'[22]

For Krogh, the simplicity of weaving is its greatest draw. 'I do not use complicated [woven] structures – I never use double weave. I am fascinated by how such a simple way [of working] can make a new material. In many new textiles, it is the thread that is the very complicated thing. I don't need to add a complicated structure. I balance complicated materials with simple techniques.'[23] Her complicated materials require a light monitor, programmed to emit a range of colours, to illuminate the optical fibre. While Krogh has watched light monitors become more efficient and economical during the time she has worked with fibre optics, they continue to be an unavoidable component of the work. (In the 'Ikat' series the light monitors are conveniently hidden in boxes at

 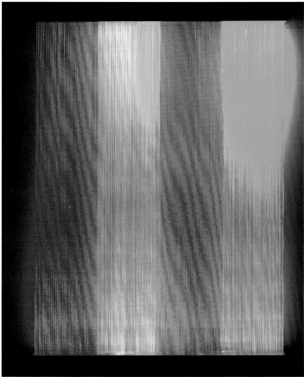

LEFT: Astrid Krogh, *Ikat I*, 2011. Fibre optic and paper weft and paper warp, plain weave hand-woven on ARM loom, 250 x 150 xm (98½ x 59 in.).

PHOTOGRAPHER: TORBEN ESKEROD

RIGHT: Astrid Krogh, *Ikat II*, 2011. Fibre optic and paper weft and paper warp, plain weave hand-woven on ARM loom, 250 x 200 cm (98½ x 78¾ in.).

PHOTOGRAPHER: TORBEN ESKEROD

the foot of the work, allowing the woven panels to hang away from the wall.) When not illuminated, the weavings are white.

'The light is the imaginary dye in "Ikat I–III"', she explains. When illuminated, colours pulse slowly through programmed sequences of shifting intensity, morphing from warm to cool light. At times the colour changes in solid blocks, elsewhere shifting in a single pick. Denmark's long, dark winters are part of Krogh's reason for working with light. 'It is essential for me to work with light because we have so little of it', she elaborates. Inspiration is found in the setting of each commission, as well as 'the exchange of materials – it could be carbon fibre or optical – but the textile relies on the same old techniques; I use plain weave. The complicated thing is the material'.

British designer **Priti Veja** creates transformable textiles. On a physical level, this means woven objects that can move from two to three dimensions; on an aesthetic level, this means surfaces with qualities that change in relation to light. Veja's hand-woven *Light Flow*, from 2006, incorporates cellophane, phosphorescent lurex, polyester yarn and an electroluminescent light cable. The range of materials included in the work make use of three types of light. The first is electroluminescent light powered by electricity. The second, phosphorescent

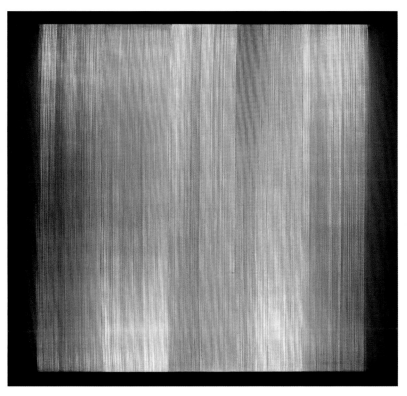

yarn, emits light after exposure to UV rays. The final source, Veja explains, is 'the natural colour and reflective properties in the weave. Plastics [such as cellophane] give transparency or play with levels of opacity to create different lighting consistencies'.[24]

Veja initially found electroluminescent materials too brittle to weave as weft and instead wove a double cloth in which the cabling can be held. The electroluminescent light cable emits two colours, with one colour transitioning slowly into the next so that 'It looks like a constant flow of light. The transition is slow, much like a flow and the lighting dims from bright light to low.' Even without a power source to control the electroluminescent cable, other materials in *Light Flow* will shift and change. When exposed to UV light, the phosphorescent thread in the weave changes colour. The difference is negligible in daylight, adding a further dimension to the work when viewed in darkness. The cellophane weft catches natural light. Like many of the examples in this chapter, *Light Flow* is a hybrid of high-tech and low-tech that makes use of both natural and artificial light – combined in one piece of woven cloth. Veja echoes Krogh when she explains, 'Weaving is very traditional – it is one of the most fundamental textile construction techniques

LEFT: Astrid Krogh, *Ikat III*, 2011. Fibre optic and paper weft and paper warp, plain weave hand-woven on ARM loom, 250 x 250 cm (98½ x 98½ in.).
PHOTOGRAPHER: TORBEN ESKEROD

RIGHT: Astrid Krogh, *Ikat II* (detail), 2011. Fibre optic and paper weft and paper warp, plain weave hand-woven on ARM loom.
PHOTOGRAPHER: TORBEN ESKEROD

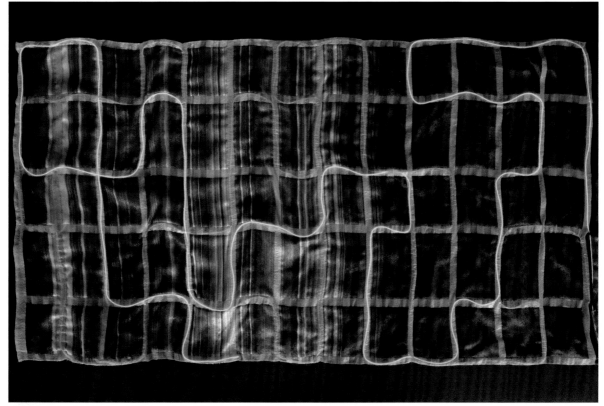

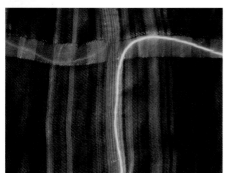

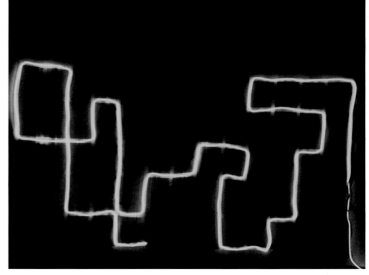

ABOVE Priti Veja, *Light Flow*, 2006 (details below). Cellophane, phosphorescent Lurex, polyester yarn and electroluminescent light cable weft and cellophane warp, hand-woven double cloth on an ARM loom, 56 x 110 cm (22 x 43¼ in.). PHOTOGRAPHER: TORIL BRANCHER

— but you really can do more with weaving by using modern technologies and modern materials. The challenge is to use the historical technique but for innovative possibilities.'

Run by June Swindell, the British company **Salt** 'focus[es] on how light filters through fabrics into spaces, creating singular optical effects without compromising the need for privacy'.[25] Over almost two decades, the company has built up a loyal following of clients who have responded to the subtle aesthetic Salt uses to create window coverings and space dividers. Designing woven screening fabrics has allowed Swindell to take structural and material risks that applications such as upholstery fabric, which face regular abrasion, cannot withstand. For example, long surface floats suggestive of water are a trademark of the collection. So too is the use of materials such as stainless steel and bronze, which require hand production, but have the added benefit of changing reflective qualities from daylight to darkness.[26] Viscose is another fibre of choice because it is lightfast and does not rot when exposed to sunlight, a crucial requirement of curtain fabrics and blinds.

Salt, *Alternate Longitude*, 2009. Stainless-steel weft and cotton and viscose warp, hand-woven on a Dobby loom.

PHOTOGRAPHER: MATTHEW JUDD

45

Salt, *Alternate Longitude* (detail), 2009. Stainless-steel weft and cotton and viscose warp, hand-woven on a Dobby loom.

'I was keen to produce a product, not a textile', Swindell explains of her initial interest in developing blinds.[27] Large commissions are constructed as panels and she has come to accept the realities of woven production and comments that 'I don't try to hide width restrictions imposed by the loom'. Even in the stormy economy of recent years, her market tends to be in North America, in part because Europe 'needs blinds less because so many buildings already have an existing system of shutters or external awnings'. Swindell's use of light is both bespoke and low-tech, but two factors suggest that blinds to screen light and for privacy will continue to be in demand: 'Our summers are getting hotter and urban living is more and more crowded, with everyone overlooking another space.'

A final example of light-based work is by Welsh artist **Ainsley Hillard**, whose weavings, like those of Salt, play with light and shadow. Hillard's 2008 'Traces' exhibition at the Mission Gallery in Swansea included 20 monochrome hand-woven panels and an audio track of steps walking around the room, the sound of writing and a bell tolling in the apse of the now deconsecrated seamen's chapel that the gallery occupies. Hillard's ghostly weavings of knitted viscose and monofilament are based on photographs she takes and enlarges to create what she describes as both a 'broken image' and one that she 'can control'. Earlier work, by her own admission, focused on the figurative and self-referential, often 're-weaving the self'.[28] More recent explorations have become less figurative and tend to explore a more generic self (admittedly, always female) in relation to space.

Hillard volunteers: 'Whilst the image is fragmented in the structure of the cloth, the position of each woven textile in the installation space is also important as it further fragments the images, and it is only by moving and locating oneself in certain positions that images come to the fore. This bodily movement enacts the very process of weaving, a rhythmic interaction with the space.'[29]

Ainsley Hillard, *Traces*, 2008–9. Audio textile installation, viscose weft and nylon monofilament warp, hand-woven plain weave, Jack loom. Mission Gallery, Wales.

PHOTOGRAPHER: JASON INGRAM

ABOVE AND OPPOSITE:
Ainsley Hillard, *Traces*
(details), 2008–9. Audio
textile installation,
viscose weft and nylon
monofilament warp, hand-
woven plain weave, Jack
loom. Mission Gallery,
Wales.

PHOTOGRAPHER: JASON INGRAM

Angela Maddock describes her first-hand experience of the work: 'As Hillard weaves so do we: passing between the warp threads, seen and lost, present and absent, weft wrapping warp, hidden and revealed. In our passing, we gather different sightings: the hazy edges, soft focus: the underbelly of the weave, normally hidden from view, is apparent for all to see, and, like the lines of a book, we notice that one pass is printed and the next is not.'[30] During installation, the front and back of the work are given equal importance, essentially removing the usefulness of these categories. Hillard sees the strategy as a way to allow the viewer to contemplate the space of the weaving within the larger space of the gallery and, as Maddock observes, 'reminds us that space is a dynamic thing and that like shadows, traces are both followed and left behind'.[31]

CHAPTER THREE

Motion

WOVEN TEXTILES MOVE AND CHANGE FOR A NUMBER OF REASONS. Some are connected to electrical circuits; others react to changes in the local environment such as temperature or humidity. Still others harbour instinctive material memory that draws them back to their original shapes. Movement can be mechanical – the result of flexibility or materials with contrasting properties, or triggered by the presence of electronic circuits. While enthusiasm for wearable technology seen in the past two decades has been tempered with pragmatism for the challenges of industrial collaboration, there exists a renewed engagement with the poetic potential of woven textiles. These woven structures make use of complex technologies, as well as the most basic inherent material properties, to become mechanically and electrically dynamic.

In the 1990s, dialogue with the Toronto craft community and specifically the Textile Museum of Canada sparked Canadian architect **Philip Beesley**'s interest in textiles. Geotextiles and netting offer the very basic approaches that underpin his experimental architectural work today. Recent investigations are part of the 'Hylozoic' series and refer to the concept of hylozism, 'an ancient belief that all matter has life'.[1] They exist as pulsing, vibrating, twitching environments capable of enveloping the viewer. Beesley's installation at the Canada Pavilion of the Venice Biennale in 2010 was described as: 'An artificial forest made of an intricate lattice of small, transparent acrylic meshwork links, covered with a network of interactive mechanical fronds, filters and whiskers. Tens of thousands of lightweight, digitally fabricated components are fitted with microprocessors and proximity sensors that react to human presence. This responsive environment functions like a giant lung that breathes in and out around its occupants.'[2]

These moving, ever-changing environments take architecture away from the permanent stuff of stone and cement and suggest in its place a future of porous boundaries capable of adaptation. 'I think woven structures can readily be described as a basis for the current work', Beesley declares. 'This work developed out of an extended dialogue with the master textile artist Warren Seelig, starting 15 years ago. In the 'Hylozoic' series, we're using a corrugated

OPPOSITE: Philip Beesley, 'Breathing Column' from *Hylozoic Soil* (detail), 2010. Laser-cut acrylic, mylar, latex, metals, custom electronics, 6m x 15m x 5m (6½ x 16½ x 5½ yd), Festival de Mexico.
PHOTO © PBAI; PHOTOGRAPHER: PIERRE CHARRON

ABOVE: Philip Beesley, *Hylozoic Grove*, 2008. Laser-cut acrylic, Mylar, latex, metals, custom electronics, 4 x 10 x 3 m (13 ft 1 in. x 32 ft 10 in. x 9 ft 9½ in.), Ars Electronica Centre, Linz, Austria.

PHOTO: © PBAI

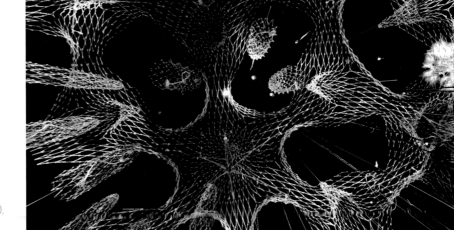

Philip Beesley, *Hylozoic Soil* (detail: overhead view), 2010. Festival de Mexico.

PHOTO: © PBAI

diagrid meshwork … acting out the same paths as fibres within a coarsely woven textile arranged on the bias … I was searching for a flexible, "live" hand to the fabric where the material could span while still being capable of draping.'[3]

Early works by Beesley's team were constructed by hand with pliers and small tools, but confronted what he terms 'a cruel disparity of scale'.[4] Digital fabrication methods helped solve his extremely labour-intensive work. He is quick to admit that a shift in perspective around the potential of digital fabrication contributed to his research. 'The idea that the digital is insensitive and soulless turns out not to be the case at all,' he confides, 'there is a lovely physicality to it.' Because digital fabrication now plays such a central role in making the work, material choices are restricted. 'Selection of polymers and sheet goods tends to be driven by compatibility with the machinery. This new craft has a restricted range, but it is also tremendously enabling.'

Are these constructions alive – or semi-living? Beesley returns to cloth, explaining: 'Think of cloth as sensitive to the influence of the body and environment. There are three kinds of activity in our installations, each relating to textiles in particular ways and each moving progressively closer to definitions of life. First is a receiving function, akin to the way a gauze veil might float around the body of the wearer. In the same way that the draping function of a textile can be described as having a particular hand, our meshworks float and move in response to their surroundings, flexing with physical contact with viewers and to local movements of air. Second is an active, mechanical response where components operate in kinetic patterns. This response combines artificial intelligence and electrically driven mechanisms. It involves a dense meshwork of miniature components, arranged in complex interlocking tileworks that we design by using textile-based ordering systems. These include arrayed microprocessors organised like an organic neural net, integrated with gridded physical components. The flexible interlinking components employ tightly-nested tessellation patterns and tartan-gridded wiring and structural fibre organisations in densely woven arrays. Third, near-living chemical metabolisms are now being integrated into the environment, supported by artificial-life laboratories in the UK and Denmark. These fluid circulation systems operate by depositing delicate layers of material and by building up felted skins. These are currently housed within glass containers that run throughout the environments. With more development, we're hoping that fibres made from these chemical reactions can cover the meshworks and function as self-renewing architectural envelopes that can change and decay with the seasons.'

Describing general design principles that guide his project, Beesley says: 'The component meshworks are deliberately weak and fragile – they are designed to share and shed their forces. Directly like the intermeshed structures of a woven textile, the system gains resiliency and strength by densely combining many small elements. Temperature, human occupation and environmental cycles all directly work on these sensitive components and the materials soak up that influence.'

Beesley respects the fact that it is a 'sympathetic viewer' who understands these responsive settings as intelligent, but posits that the reasons to pursue such poetic challenges are in fact quite tangible. They can enhance and support the environment as a cooperative layer in much the same way as we see geotextiles stabilising soil erosion. They can work to capture and process carbon in a way similar to that of a filter or lymph system. But as experimental forms, they are what he readily terms a 'mongrel space' and warns that these magical environments are currently 'far from equilibrium'.

At the opposite end of the technology spectrum, Dutch designer **Maria Blaisse** experiments with the same chevron structure that underpins Beesley's environments by using bamboo to create flexible forms. Several years ago, Blaisse attended an exhibition in the Netherlands, organised to promote the use of bamboo, and observed that designers were not exploring the material's natural flexibility. 'My studio for the past seventeen years is surrounded by a bamboo fence,' she explains, 'and I see the beautiful material bending gracefully every day in the weather.'[5] Blaisse has worked for decades with the simple form of the inner tube of a tyre, moving this one basic starting point between two and three dimensions to generate a surprising diversity of final shapes. As she began exploring the potential of bamboo, using mesh structures she had first learned 30 years earlier while travelling in South America, she noticed an uncanny similarity in the forms that were emerging. 'I was totally surprised again: the inner tube of car tyres is a basic structure that opens up to anything. I can make it two-dimensional or three-dimensional in different ways and movement is always in it.'

Blaisse works closely with professional dancers to study the potential forms her flexible structures can offer. 'A lot of things that happen in nature become visible when you dance and move with it', she avers. She does not instruct the dancers in their movement, but rather works with dancers who are capable of improvisation and are 'conscious of form and sensitive to construction'. The thickness and proportion of the bamboo mesh is precisely balanced to enable the forms to move freely in all directions. These studies are currently scaled to the human body. The next step is on a larger scale, with the aim of flexibility for architectural-scale pavilions. 'Surface becomes a volume', she notes of a constant theme throughout her design work. 'My work is always about volume and movement, the material is always in movement and changing form.'

Maria Blaisse, 'Moving Meshes' series, 2008 and ongoing. Hand-plaited bamboo mesh, movement study. PHOTOGRAPHER: MARIA BLAISSE

Barbara Layne, a Canadian-American researcher based in Montreal, has worked at the forefront of electronic textiles for the past decade. She is a founding member of Hexagram at the Institute for Research and Creation in Media Arts and Technologies, based at Concordia University in Montreal. Her research makes use of LEDs, microcomputers and sensors to create textiles for performance and art that respond to external stimuli. 'I love the logistics of weaving with the X- and Y-axis. This is parallel to how a circuit works … Most people talk about the binary [similarity between weaving and computing], but for me it is the grid.'[6] The *Black and White Dress* currently in development contains the largest LED display Layne has worked with yet: 384 lights in total. Using any device that contains Bluetooth – such as a smartphone or computer – you can send a text- or graphics-based message and it will be displayed on the dress. The number of characters is limited, which encourages the use of short messages, but Layne points out that animations or scrolling designs can be sent, which 'takes texting to another level'.

OPPOSITE: Barbara Layne, *Black and White Dress* by Studio subTela, 2011 (detail above). White linen and hand-woven yellow LEDs; new images sent wirelessly to the dress.

PHOTOGRAPHER: HESAM KHOSHNEVISS

The research, Layne explains, 'is certainly not limited to the dress' as a platform. Curtains, Layne offers as an alternative, could change to suit the situation of a social gathering. But fashion holds a certain appeal: 'For me, it is always fun to make [electronic textiles] into clothing. What happens when people become involved? Wearable communication is about surprising yourself.' What does restrict the work is cost. Rock bands and Olympic teams have both approached Layne to discuss commissions, but currently cost prohibits the production of multiples. 'There is still so much hand work – every garment has 150 hours or more of hand craft.' Layne notes that recent availability of LEDs manufactured with holes that can be sewn through (rather than hard legs which have to be removed) can be used in both weaving and embroidery and are 'cutting making time in half'. While smaller components and smarter materials are emerging, 'connection and adaptation of electronic components is where the hand work comes in'. This is a challenge faced by many others, including Zane Berzina's *E-Static Shadows* project.

Zane Berzina in collaboration
with architect Jackson Tan,
E-Static Shadows (detail),
2007–9. Hand-woven triple
layer cloth with LEDs,
Jacquard loom.

PHOTOGRAPHER: VILNIS LAPINS

Latvian artist **Zane Berzina**'s *E-Static Shadows* project (2007–9), realised in collaboration with architect Jackson Tan, TITV, Greiz – The Institute for Special Textiles and Flexible Materials (DE) and Goldsmiths Digital Studios (UK), harnesses static electricity. 'There are waves of energy around us that we don't know about. In fact we are constantly generating considerable amounts of static energy ourselves just by ordinary everyday interactions with our environment and the various materials surrounding us … Electrostatic energy is not visible or otherwise noticeable by human senses (except in extremely high voltages), but it still exists', Berzina states.[7] The project created an electronic textile that allowed viewers to listen and play with their own static electricity. 'They plug themselves into the installation, [and] become part of the circuit', she explains, and while wearing headphones can 'hear white noise, electricity passing through conductive threads'. As the viewer interacts with the cloth, electrostatic charges manipulate the sound feedback, making it stronger or weaker. 'The luminous e-textile membrane is always on by default – the LEDs of the soft e-textile matrix are addressed individually and get switched off in places where the membrane registers static charges, thus creating visual feedback or an "electrostatic shadow".'[8]

Berzina explains that '[The installation] encourages an intuitive interaction between the viewer and the material space, due to its purely analogue set-up. The unmediated body is the sole trigger of the audiovisual feedback, and this interaction is in no way manipulated or enhanced through digital processing,

thus allowing for genuine and very subtle differentiations in the visitor's sensory experiences.'[9] However, encouraging the public's interest in static electricity required an explanation. Without this, Berzina acknowledges, 'some were scared of the work, and some thrilled'. Because the amounts and intensity of static charge are based on the environment (dryness of the air as well as materials used in the interior), and the material properties of textiles worn by the visitors, the exhibition space often requires fine-tuning to become statically positive, for example by laying synthetic carpet, which enhances the charging-up process. A dry climate also emphasises the effect.

For the communication of the project's intentions, Berzina reveals that 'We really wanted a high-quality Jacquard weave. The brocade feel and the matt shine of the different weights of silver-coated conductive threads offer a precious look and at the same time the dense weave structure protects the electronic circuits, which are so fragile.' A triple-layer cloth was used in the final version, which ultimately allowed it to be more functional because circuits could be fully integrated. Hours of labour were required to create the individual circuits for each LED that allowed each separate transistor to react independently to the environment. 'One cut in the wrong place and the whole cloth is wasted', Berzina warns. These challenges were, in part, aesthetically determined. 'We wanted to work with the smallest LEDs and transistors physically possible to solder, so the entire e-textile system looks and feels cloth-like'. Like so many experiences that bring electronics and textiles together, the technical innovation

Zane Berzina in collaboration with architect Jackson Tan, *E-Static Shadows* (detail), 2007–9.

PHOTOGRAPHER: VILNIS LAPINS

was made real by hand. Students assisted with some of the work, but 'out of your hands other people make mistakes', Berzina observes of the project's exacting nature.

Berzina echoes the opinions voiced by other researchers, such as Christine Keller and Maggie Orth, when she states the importance of not overcomplicating technology. 'The human body is the real trigger and nothing is manipulated. Digital systems allow you to think you trigger something, but in fact you don't have control over that. But this is not a digital system. It is a purely analogue system. The body and static charges are reflected on the cloth [accompanied by] sound feedback. We didn't manipulate anything.'

American **Maggie Orth**, of International Fashion Machines, explains: 'Weaving allows you to make multi-layers with structures that are theoretically similar to a circuit. It also allows you to lay out circuits very finely, either with [a] computer or hand-weaving.'[10] Working with double-weave structures and thermochromic ink, Orth uses drive electronics to send electric currents to different parts of her woven fabrics. This heats the fabric and causes colour change. With programming, she can control when different parts of the fabric change colour. She outlines the way it works: 'The weave structure can directly interact with software and create events in time. In double weave, areas of colour will change first because the yarn is near the top. Later, the yarns on the back of the structure will cause colour change. This is an event in time that is a result of the cloth structure. The beauty is being able to reveal things about the weave structure that we cannot necessarily see. For example, as the conductive yarns move in and out [of the woven structure] and are then printed over, their journey will not be visible until heat is introduced.'

'The title of *100 Electronic Art Years* refers to the ambiguous lifetime of colour-change textiles, and all electronic art. All electronic art fails, all art fails. The question is how, and with what result. As with all colour-change textiles, the bright colours will eventually become permanently burned into the surface of the piece, creating a permanent record of software and physical artefact. When asked how long each piece will continue to perform, I can only answer in "electronic art years".'[11] Positioning her research in the worlds of art and design, she notes that one of the most satisfying responses she has received is from viewers who tell her, 'I don't understand modern art, but I like this.' She comments that weaving 'takes a lot of work and people respect that. Weaving gives the sense of being finished, well crafted and well put together, as opposed to sloppy, and can give polish to a piece', and adds 'I can make circuits in fabric because I can control where the conductive yarns go, but the reality of making a woven circuit is more difficult.' She concedes that the creation of electronic textiles is 'something like a black art, it is like cooking, something you have to do over and over again'.

Maggie Orth, *100 Electronic Art Years* (detail), 2009. Hand-woven cotton, rayon, conductive yarns, double weave with silver ink, thermochromic ink, drive electronics and software.

PHOTOGRAPHER: DAVID CLUGSTON

BELOW: Maggie Orth, *100 Electronic Art Years*, 2009. Hand-woven cotton, rayon, conductive yarns, double weave with silver ink, thermochromic ink, drive electronics and software, 157.5 x 137.2 x 20.3 cm (62 x 54 x 8 in.).

PHOTOGRAPHER: DAVID CLUGSTON

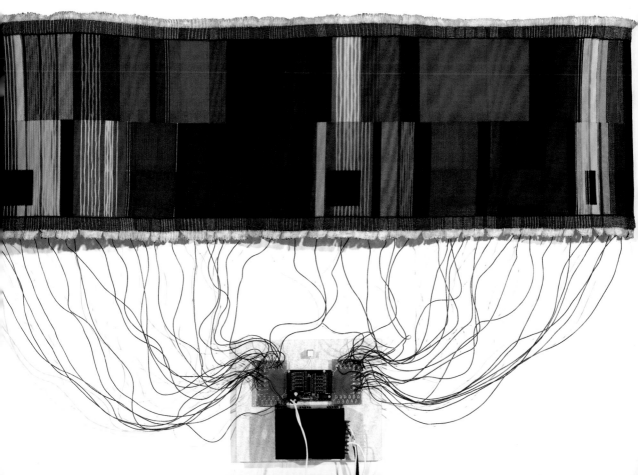

Elaine Ng Yan Ling, from Techno Naturology, 'LUX' collection (detail), 2010. Metallic yarn, shape memory yarn, polyester and wool weft and polyester warp, triple cloth on Jacquard loom.

PHOTOGRAPHER: ELAINE NG YAN LING

While designers and artists who have devoted decades to the exploration of electronic textiles are acutely aware of the challenges facing the field, students continue to take up the subject. Priorities have shifted for many, as British designer **Elaine Ng Yan Ling** explains of her recent 'Naturology' collection developed while a student at Central Saint Martin's College of Art and Design in London. She cites a merging of craft and technology in her work, but 'highlighting technology is not the key aim'.[12] 'The digital world has improved so much, it is not new any more. The craft element to my work means still trying to be carefully considered in design. Weaving is a traditional craft skill, but needs to be updated, which is why I have a weave element within all my designs.'

Ng's 'Naturology' collection refers to 'using artificial technology to activate and stimulate nature's technology in order to create a tectonic movement. The word "tectonic" might be associated with geographic movement, but within the context of techno "Naturology", the definition of "tectonic" is when the behaviour of nature subtly weaves back into the urban landscape'. She employs a number of strategies to generate movement in her work. Metal yarns in the form of shape memory alloys are subject to an electric current that generates movement. Proximity and humidity sensors are also used to create movement. She has learnt that the less stable the woven structure, the more opportunity is created for the weft yarn to grow, expand and move. Essentially, the same electrical current, when passed through different materials, provokes different responses generating motion over time.

Ng's experiments have not been without setbacks. 'The alloy produces a lot of heat and sets fire to fibres, which is a constraint in weaving', she chuckles. 'Similarly, polyester has a shape memory and is heat-sensitive, but at a much lower temperature.' Experiments with wood veneer and cane, which are sensitive to moisture levels in the air, allow the cane to be folded and moulded into organic shapes. For example, weaving with strips of printed balsa wood means that when the material changes temperature over time, it expands and contracts. This movement creates gaps in the woven structure, which in turn alter the shadows cast by the work.

Yet another low-tech, but structurally challenging, way to create a dynamic woven textile is through the potential of the woven structure for pleating, folding and bending. In 2006, the British designer **Lucy McMullen** wove *Maelstrom*, a multi-layered pleated structure loosely inspired by the American author Edgar Alan Poe's 1841 short story 'A Descent Into the Maelstrom', for the launch of the ASF Shetland organisation in Scotland. Poe sets his story on the north-west coast of Norway and describes 'an event such as never happened before to mortal man'.[13] The fictional event Poe imagines is a giant whirlpool and the notion of this imaginary structure and its 'twisting sense permeated my thoughts', McMullen explains, before adding that the golden ratio and the Fibonacci number sequence offered further inspiration.

McMullen studied embroidered and woven textiles at Glasgow School of Art and then focused on woven textiles at the Royal College of Art in London.

LEFT: Elaine Ng Yan Ling, from Techno Naturology, 'LUX' collection (detail), 2010. Metallic yarn and balsa wood weft and cellophane warp, hand-woven on Dobby loom, with shape-memory polymers.
PHOTOGRAPHER: ELAINE NG YAN LING

RIGHT: Elaine Ng Yan Ling, from Techno Naturology, *The Flapper* (detail), 2010. Chair cane, wool, polyester and shape memory yarn weft, and wool and cellophane warp, pleated double cloth hand-woven on Dobby loom.
PHOTOGRAPHER: ELAINE NG YAN LING

Lucy McMullen, *Maelstrom*, 2006. Shetland wool warp and silk spun cord with a copper core weft, three-section multi-layered pleat, hand-woven on 24-shaft computerised AVL loom, 120 x 30 cm (47¼ x 11¾ in.).

PHOTOGRAPHER: KEN MCBRIDE

She attributes her participation in multidisciplinary collaborations with vehicle and industrial design students at the RCA to her 'thinking beyond just fabric'.[14] She now teaches at the University of Ulster in Belfast, Northern Ireland and declares, 'I like to make people think about the broader picture of weaving. There is a lot you can do with structure and the potential of weave. It does not need to be fabric – it could be used for engineering or even architectural applications. But it is the basics that are important. I wouldn't be able to do anything if I did not *understand* what I was doing. I tell students to put down the textbooks. They are fine as reference, but if you are merely reproducing, you are never going to be groundbreaking.'[15] In her own design work, she admits to being 'obsessed with volume. I am trying to get away from the regimented format and traditional view of what you think you can do with weaving'.

Maelstrom was woven in three sections on a warp of Shetland wool with a weft of silk spun cord with a copper core to give the work its structural integrity, and starched after weaving to preserve the crisp edges. The sections allow the work to be folded flat for transport and storage – a requirement of the original brief set by the foundation. The work is intended for display on the floor, so that the viewer is peering down into the swirling vortex of a woven whirlpool. Despite the structural complexity of the work, McMullen admits that the multi-layered pleats were in fact the 'most straightforward' of her ideas for the commission. She places specific requirements on her weaving: 'Retaining the unique aspects of weaving is what I centre around. Weaving is such an intense process – it has to be something that can't be done any other way. I like the way weaving makes me work: the process is so methodical and demands thinking ahead – before you even go near a loom.'

British designer **Philippa Brock** describes herself as a 'woven textile design engineer' with an emphasis, in her design work, on a three-dimensional Jacquard weave structure and yarn interaction.[16] With an education in both printed and woven textiles, Brock focuses on the potential of on-loom finishing techniques – essentially just how much can be completed in the design of a woven textile before the fabric is removed from the industrial power loom. The approach can increase the efficiency of production, as well as offering more sustainable solutions because it aims to reduce the numbers of finishing steps. For example, if pleats can be engineered into the woven fabric as a result of the weave structure and choice of materials, then the fabric does not need to be pleated with separate equipment in an additional production

LEFT: Philippa Brock, *Self Fold 4* (detail), from 'Self-Fold' series, 2008. Paper, copper, and elastomeric weft and silk warp, triple layer structure, Dataweave Jacquard loom.
PHOTOGRAPHER: PHILIPPA BROCK

RIGHT: Philippa Brock, *ARR14* (detail), from 'Self Assembly' series, 2009. Polyester and elastomeric weft and cellophane warp, double/triple layer structure, Dataweave Jacquard loom.
PHOTOGRAPHER: PHILIPPA BROCK

Philippa Brock, self-assembly
initial experiments on
loom (detail), from 'Self
Assembly' series, 2008. Weft
polyester and elastomeric
and silk warp, double/triple
layer structure, Dataweave
Jacquard loom.

PHOTOGRAPHER: PHILIPPA BROCK

step after weaving. The design process relies on both analogue and digital techniques, often beginning with hand-weaving to test yarns, before moving to production on the power loom.

A recent collaborative project at Central Saint Martins College of Art and Design, where Brock is the Woven Textile Pathway Leader, brought together textile designers and scientists who have won the Nobel prize. Brock was paired with Sir Aaron Klug, who was part of the team of scientists who created three-dimensional models of viruses from two-dimensional data using X-ray crystallography: X-rays taken from multiple angles that built a three-dimensional image of the virus. This interaction between two and three dimensions continued in her work for the 'Warp Factor 09' exhibition, when Brock collaborated with the Japanese Oji paper fibre company to find new ways in which the fine paper yarn might be used. The 'Self-Fold' series was 'inspired by experimenting with paper folding techniques, through both inputting self-generated origami and layered weave structure plans … [and exploring] how woven textiles can be engineered to self-fold on vertical, horizontal and diagonal axes'.[17] 'Depending on the weave structure and yarn interaction, each yarn would self-fold when it came off [the] loom', she explains.

Off the loom, time also plays a part in these dynamic structures. Previously, Brock used elastomeric to aid the self-assembly/self-folding processes within the layering systems. In her new work, she attempts to avoid weaving with elastomeric because it degrades and can, at times, lack subtlety. Instead, she uses crêpe/high-twist yarns, so the works can continue to fold into three-dimensional forms as they respond to changes in humidity. 'I have worked with CAD and Jacquard for a long time,' Brock reflects, 'and to a certain extent I know what things are going to do. But changing the sett [such as warp/weft density] can mean something totally different happens.' She admits that alongside her considerable experience and attention to planning, her designs ultimately involve 'a certain amount of serendipity'.[18]

Research into the potential of dynamic woven textiles ranges, in this chapter, from the simplicity of hand-constructed mesh created from bamboo by Blaisse to research that continues to push the limits of electronic textiles as seen in the research of Layne. Some research strategies rely heavily on digital technologies, while others remain focused on the simplicity and control that analogue approaches can provide. Danish artist **Grethe Sørensen** increasingly moves back and forth between analogue and digital production in her explorations of 'elusive optical phenomena, colour gradations and a weave construction based on digital technology'.[19]

While the past decade has offered weavers new interdisciplinary options for developing and controlling the woven structure, a knowledge of hand-weaving remains vital to the success of many digital explorations. Sørensen declares that: 'The digital tools have given me an opening to a new world of imagery ... [building] bridges that give me access to other media where I can work and express myself. I am still rooted in woven textiles – but the combination of the two media enriches both and I draw inspiration from both, from the textiles to the video and from the video to the textiles.'[20]

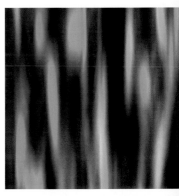

Woven on a digital Jacquard loom, the imagery for Sørensen's 2009 series, 'Millions of Colours', is based on screen grabs from animations of her earlier woven work. She explains, 'At the same time as my loom became digitised, so did the film and video equipment my husband (Bo Hovgaard) was using ... Suddenly we were working in the same media and that gave us a new possibility to work together.'[21] Working in a constant loop that moves from the manual to the digital, Sørensen starts with digitally constructed motifs that she samples as hand-weavings, before moving them to large-scale weaving on a digital Jacquard loom. These weavings become the basis of digital animations, and screenshots from the animations provide artwork for the next cycle of weavings. She comments: 'It has been inspiring to make animation. It gives something the other way.'[22]

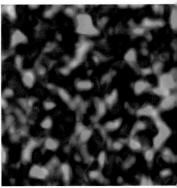

Grethe Sørensen and Bo Hovgaard, *Out of Focus*, 2007. Frame grabs of digital animation based on woven textile. Exhibited at Kunstcentret Silkeborg Bad, Denmark.

Grethe Sørensen, 'Millions of Colours' series, 2009, view from left. Cotton weft and warp, random weave structure developed by artist and woven on digital Jacquard loom. Exhibited at Rundetaarn, Copenhagen, Denmark.

PHOTOGRAPHER: BO HOVGAARD

Despite her use of digital technologies today, she explains that hand-weaving continues to be the starting point of many projects. 'I always develop my technique from an image', she says, adding that it is the 'design that dictates technique' rather than her process being determined by her tools. Her career has focused on weaving – designing for upholstery and interiors – and, like many individuals with a broad portfolio, she finds that her artistic practice feeds her more conventional design commitments. For example, work from 'Millions of Colours' is now being re-woven as a furnishing fabric at the Oriole Mill in North Carolina, with the palette reduced to four yarn colours.

The movement of industrial textile production away from Europe and North America in the past decade is often cited as a reason for a deskilled workforce, unemployment and our excessive material consumption. While these concerns are valid, Sørensen observes that this shift in production has also opened up new opportunities for independent designers. 'The decimation of the traditional weaving industry has created a never-before-accessible bridge to contemporary production machinery', she offers. 'Where large mills traditionally had emphasised long runs, small mills allow the possibility of weaving one-off products, individual design, small series and site-specific textiles etc. on industrial Jacquard looms. My work has never before been so inspiring and intensive.'[23]

But Sørensen is also cautious about the wholesale power of digital design

strategies for textiles and sees their potential only when used in combination with the hands-on knowledge she spent decades refining prior to the digital revolution. 'Designers and artists with hands in the production are the developers of new expressions. The manual work with thread and construction is essential in order to be able to play with the tactile values embedded in the textile.'[24] Along with material knowledge, working by hand provides the opportunity for chance. 'The coincidences that happen while playing with materials and constructions are invaluable and cannot be replaced by computer screens. In spite of the fact that most of my work will end up being woven on a Jacquard machine, it will always pass through my hands in the developing process – to me this sample-weaving process is essential. Even though computer programs may be able to visualise anything you can ever dream of constructing, they will never have the sensuous knowledge of your hands.'[25]

Grethe Sørensen, 'Millions of Colours' series, view from right.

CHAPTER FOUR

Sound

SOUND AND WEAVING MEET IN UNEXPECTED WAYS. Artists use the noise of industrial production as the basis of woven artwork; designers use visualisations of sound as patterns for woven cloth. Musicians and artists collaborate in a search for new woven structures, as well as new sources of music. Cassette tape provides an unconventional weft fibre. Finally, woven textiles are noted for their acoustic properties and are used to reduce noise levels. From making noise to creating silence, the binary system shared by the woven textile and audio recordings has allowed these seemingly foreign worlds come together.

American artist **Christy Matson**'s undergraduate studies focused on hand-weaving. But during visits to the remaining industrial mills of Trion, North Carolina she found herself 'blown away by the speed and noise'.[1] Postgraduate studies with Lia Cook at what is now the California College of Arts in San Francisco meant working with hand-operated Jacquard TC1 looms that run off air compressors: more noise. If weaving often evokes images of peaceful – even meditative – activity, Matson admits: 'I never go there. To weave you have to be present; it is complicated.' Crucially, she found 'The more technology is introduced, the more it becomes even less meditative, even loud.' It is this experience of the loudness of weaving that has inspired a body of work that explores the relationship between sound and cloth.

With a background in hand-weaving, Matson initially found that the possibilities of Jacquard weaving felt endless. 'All of a sudden the tool can weave anything: a picture, a pattern. All limitations are lifted with Jacquard. What do you weave?' In answering this question, she began 'examining the process [of weaving] from every angle', including creating videotapes and sound recordings. This self-reflexive approach led to an interest in feedback loops and early cybernetics. 'I wanted to involve the loom in the generation of my work. Recording the sound of the loom and making pictures of the sound of the loom allowed me to scrutinise my relationship with the tools I employ in my work.'

During a residency at the Oriole Mill in Hendersonville, North Carolina in 2009, Matson created a sound and video piece entitled *Mill Sounds*. The work was made at the time of the economic crash in the USA when Matson found

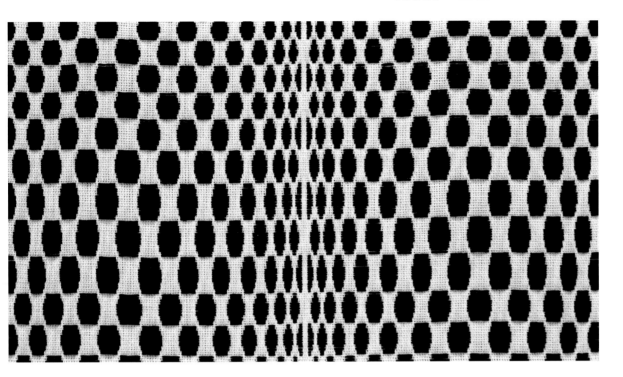

ABOVE: Christy Matson, *Composition in Circles: White* (detail), 2011. Cotton weft and warp hand woven on a Macomber loom.

PHOTOGRAPHER: MATTHEW MILLER

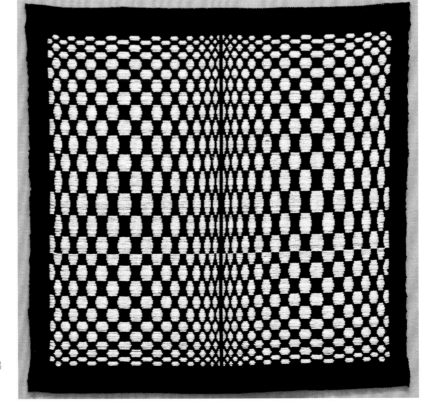

Christy Matson, *Composition in Circles: Black*, 2011. Cotton weft and warp hand woven on a Macomber loom, 45.7 x 45.7 cm (18 x 18 in.).

PHOTOGRAPHER: MATTHEW MILLER

Christy Matson, *Composition in Circles: White* and *Composition in Circles: Black*, 2011. Cotton weft and warp hand-woven on a Macomber loom and record player. Installation view, *Laurie Herrick: Weaving Yesterday, Today and Tomorrow*, Museum of Contemporary Craft in partnership with Pacific Northwest College of Art, USA.

PHOTOGRAPHER: MATTHEW MILLER

herself questioning the logic of 'weaving a massive yardage' at such a precarious time in financial history. 'Instead of creating all this cloth', she explains, a one-minute audio clip of the industrial loom at work was stretched over an hour. The work considered 'time, hand and industrial production' and quite unlike what Matson experienced within the mill, the audio becomes 'meditative as the sound changes and evolves over the course of an hour'.

Matson does not have a musical background and confesses that she cannot play an instrument. A computer, handily, translates sound files into weave structures, adapted to 'fit into the matrix width of the loom I am working on'. As a result, pixels of the sound file become threads of cloth. In 2011, a two-week residency at the Museum of Contemporary Craft in Portland, Oregon gave her time to respond to the weavings of Portland weaver Laurie Herrick, who worked from the 1960s through to the 1990s with overshot structures to create optical patterns. 'I became interested in how Herrick's geometric patterned structures might relate to a musical composition', she explains, in particular the 'horizontal and vertical fading in and out of squares'.[2] Matson first uploaded a photograph of Herrick's weaving into her Metasynth software program. The software allows the user to control how an image is read both horizontally and vertically in relation to parameters such as tempo and scale. 'Any picture could generate hundreds of sonic outputs', Matson explains. Two woven versions were then developed, one with a black background and one with a white background. Referencing the visual coding of sound, Matson explains that sound editing uses black pixels to equate with silence and white to equate with sound. The resulting pair of works could be understood as loud and quiet – translating the 'visual sensibility' of sound is Matson's priority.

Rather than engineer the textile to emit sound as she has done in earlier work, Matson physically separated the two elements (sound and weaving) of the final exhibition. The scores for the white-and-black weavings were cut on two sides of a record, labelled simply with a white-and-black coloured sticker, and placed on a record player near the weavings in the gallery. 'I wanted sound present, but not so directly. Each weaving as an image could stand on its own, the same as [the audio on] the record player. The weaving and recording are in the same space for the viewer to make the connection, or to not make that connection.'

Much like Matson, **Lars Preisser** has responded to the noise of industrial weaving. Preisser's family worked as engineers on industrial looms during his childhood in Germany, giving him exposure at a young age to the speed, but also the volume, of industrial textile production. Today he weaves by hand on a computer-aided loom, one relatively quiet extreme in the spectrum of options for woven production. Repetition is an ongoing inquiry, from the 'repetitive movement of both the machine and me as the weaver, in addition structures and patterns mirror that repetition and finally the sound of weaving … repetitious as well'.[3]

For *Weaving With the Sound of Its Own Making*, Preisser wove a black cloth containing a stereo cable transmitting a recording of the sound of the cloth as it was woven. He acknowledges that the sculptor Robert Morris worked with a similar concept for his *Box With the Sound of Its Own Making* in 1961, creating an object capable of emitting the noise of its own creation. Preisser describes his own version: 'The stereo cable which is woven through the fabric in regular intervals is actually transporting the sound of the weaving alongside the visual sound and gives the listener an insight into the process of weaving, echoing its own creation.'

Lars Preisser, *Weaving With The Sound of Its Own Making*, (detail below), 2009. Wool, cotton and audio cable weft on cotton warp, summer and winter weave structure hand woven on a 24-shaft AVL Compu-Dobby loom. Exhibited at the Blue Oyster Gallery, Dunedin, New Zealand.

PHOTOGRAPHER: LARS PREISSER

Lars Preisser, *Weaving With The Sound of Its Own Making*, 2009. Wool, cotton and audio cable weft on cotton warp, summer and winter weave structure hand-woven on a 24 shaft AVL Compu-Dobby loom. Exhibited at Objectspace, Auckland, New Zealand.
PHOTOGRAPHER: LARS PREISSER

'Weaving can be seen as a time-based medium, as music is, but at the same time visible as a whole in its finished state. But it is also that finished state I doubt. It would be simple-minded to reduce it to the process only too. That is why I implemented the process into the piece in the form of the sound. The pattern of the weaving shows the audio waveform of the sound, which makes the progress of the sound and weaving visible.' Rather than fill the gallery with sound that viewers could not control, the audio element of the installation was fed through headphones. Preisser adds that the headphones also offer a reference back to his childhood mill visits, when 'everyone had to wear ear protection'. 'Instead of blocking out information', he explains, the headphones 'reverse that earlier experience'.

A three-year collaboration starting in 2005 between the Danish musician and songwriter **Hanne Raffnsøe** and artist **Lise Frølund** found the pair asking each other, 'Can we make the loom sing?' and, in return, 'Can we give body to the song?'[4] 'The platform of our joint project was that music and weaving share basically the same code, which becomes apparent when music is recorded and weavings are carried out with single thread control', Frølund explains of the work that became *Let the Weave Sing, and Let the Music Materialise*.[5] The concept of the project was based on the same binary information being read by the 'wrong' reader to allow music to be woven, and woven structures to become sound.

Lise Frølund and Hanne Raffnsøe, *LULLALOOM: Let the Weave Sing, and Let the Music Materialise*, 2008. Installation of plywood music box and a draining tray, cardboard punch cards, synthesiser and woven textiles, Officinet Gallery, Copenhagen, Denmark.

PHOTOGRAPHER: OLE AKHØJ

Working with the IT specialist Anna Buskgaard, the pair developed a computer program that allowed data from sound files to be allocated to the woven structure. 'Our sound file consisted of 16 bits, which is to say that each sound registration appeared graphically as 16 digits (0s and 1s) in succession. The next line of digits was placed directly below the first one, etc. Music is recorded with 44.400 Hz registrations per second. This way we got an extremely long punched card: 16 warp threads and as many weft threads as we could possibly manage.'[6] In reality the sound data translated into an enormous volume of weaving: Raffnsøe's lullaby of less than one minute in duration became 27 m (29½ yd) of wool cloth woven by Frølund. Structurally, the translation of the music into weaving also created long wool floats on the face of the fabric, which were machine-washed to encourage felting after weaving. The cloth was then cut down into individual blankets.

'We also said, what if we want to weave cloth that works well? A 1/12 satin weave structure was added on top of the lullaby to weave a long shawl.'[7] The new hybrid structure was then 'converted back to music as a mix of weave structure and lullaby'. Plain weave, twill and satin variations were all tested as potential sound, but Frølund admits that many of these structures were 'not interesting from a musician's point of view' and, crucially, the project had to work equally between the two artists. For the exhibition at Officinet, the gallery of the Danish Crafts Association in Copenhagen, a traditional music box was included to encourage viewers to see, and hear, the connection between the punch cards used to create music and those used to control the woven structure on the loom. Frølund explains that the traditional music box with cleverly hidden synthesiser was displayed with board cards and a hole punch, so viewers could cut their own punch cards and 'turn them through the music box and manipulate the sound by pulling the different wooden handles on top of the box, which were attached to the synthesiser. This had of course nothing to do with our method of dogmatic translation between weave and sound, but was a visualisation of the process'.[8] While the collaboration has shown the pair what sound and weaving share, Frølund is firm in her commitment to weaving: 'The loom is full enough of challenges', she states. 'I would never do anything that is not a challenge, but I do not find the complex interesting.' Instead she cites the moment when complexity returns to simplicity as her recurring goal.

Norwegian artist **Elin Igland** was similarly interested in the potential for collaboration between weaving and music. Igland trained as a weaver at the Bergen National Academy of the Arts and is currently a postgraduate student at the Art Academy in Oslo. Like many artists in this chapter, Igland found the shared binary system and the noise of weaving on the TC1 Jacquard loom (which happens to be manufactured in Norway) led her to start considering the connections that could be made between sound and weaving. Working

with a white wool warp and weft, Igland hand-wove a fabric that contained 88 LEDs and connected one light to each key on the piano below to create *Pattern Examination of Sound No. 1: Piano* in 2009. Her intention is to create a 'pattern machine' that will allow an archive of sound patterns to be collected over time.[9] 'When the different lights are glowing, they work as filled squares in a grid, which by photographing, gets to be a new pattern in a new woven textile later on. That way, I collect an archive of patterns over time, which is created by the different musicians playing on the piano', Igland reveals.[10]

The 'white weaving for a white cube' was planned to allow the textile to become part of the background of the environment. During performances in the dark, viewers enjoy a moving pattern of illuminated LEDs that dance across the woven panel above the piano. The type of music played dictates the visual pattern of lights, which seem to sparkle in the air. In the future, Igland plans to create woven textiles based on the light patterns created during performances that use the piano/weaving. 'There is a never-ending investigation of how different musicians create different patterns. Will a classical pianist create different patterns than a piano player that plays jazz? What about improvisational music? Or four-handed?'

RIGHT AND OPPOSITE:
Elin Igland, *Pattern Examination of Sound No. 1: Piano*, 2009. Wool warp and weft, hand-woven plain weave, piano, cables, electronic components.
PHOTOGRAPHER, IMAGE RIGHT: PETER KLASSON; PHOTOGRAPHER, IMAGE OPPOSITE: ALETTE SCHEI RØRVIK

American artist **Alyce Santoro**'s *Silent (dress)*, part of her 'Sonic Fabric' collection, is made of cassette tape ribbon woven on a black polyester warp.[11] '"Sonic Fabric" was originally intended solely for use in installation artworks based on the notion, common to both Buddhism and quantum physics, that at the most basic level, everything in the universe may consist of little more than vibration.'[12] The project is inspired by Santoro's childhood memories of learning to sail, when cassette tape was used as a wind indicator on the boat's rigging. Later in life, she learnt that Tibetan prayer flags silkscreened with music are believed to send music out on the wind. Santoro is a musician in her own right – a flute player – and makes sound art. The cassette tape ribbon she uses 'mixes together sounds from the world, from Tibetan monks to Beethoven'.[13] She makes it clear that the work is conceptual art, rather than a sustainability gesture, pointing out that 'Cassette tape is not eco-friendly. It is toxic and doesn't degrade.' 'My life is about being sustainable,' she adds, 'I live off the grid, but the project is more about tape being a ubiquitous material that happens to contain sonic potential – this is meaningful for me.'[14]

When she first began working with recycled cassette tape, Santoro started knitting the material, but found the structure too loose, a problem solved when she wove the cassette tape ribbon as weft. Early weaving trials involved the use of individual cassette tapes; but the approach proved difficult to weave because each new tape had to be hand-tied and 30-, 60- and 90-minute tapes are all of differing thicknesses. Today the declining audiocassette book industry has left thousands of spools of unrecorded tape that Santoro has begun to work with. An open-minded family-run textile mill in New England copes with the unconventional order of weaving up the material using a 1940s Dobby loom.

We may think we live in a post-cassette tape world, but it continues to be used in 'many developing countries because it doesn't skip. It is still manufactured'. Santoro intends the project to go on for as long as possible and accepts that 'If I use [cassette tape] up, then I will be happy to end the project.' Weaving takes place in the United States to avoid outsourcing, although projects involving a Nepalese cooperative for Tibetan weavers and women weavers in Mexico are intended to develop bulk production of the fabric in future. 'The next phase is for other people to be involved', she explains. 'When other people make things out of it ['Sonic Fabric'] it means it will be taken to different levels by different people.'

But Sonic Fabric is not only about the use of an unconventional material. 'It is important what was recorded on to the tape', Santoro elaborates. After weaving, a 'patchwork' of sound can be heard by running a cassette tape head over the cloth. She likens the sound to static or a garbled, underwater audio. 'The tape folded up in fabric means the cassette head is picking up six or eight tracks of sound at one time.' Santoro describes the sound as 'strange and intricate

Alyce Santoro and seamstress Jeannette Santoro, *Silent* (dress), 2007. Pre-recorded cassette tape weft and cotton warp ('Sonic Fabric'), plain weave woven on Dobby loom.

PHOTOGRAPHER: ERIK GOULD

COURTESY OF THE MUSEUM OF ART, RHODE ISLAND SCHOOL OF DESIGN, PROVIDENCE

music made by weaving together unlikely combinations of looped and layered samples of found, created, and collected sounds'.[15]

German designer **Drahomira Hampl** provides another example of cassette tape used as weft. 'I am not particularly interested in recycled materials,' she admits, 'but I had easy access to old, broken music cassette tapes, as many people do. I like to experiment and I like to use unusual materials that you wouldn't expect to find in textiles, as a substitute for familiar yarns.'[16] The result is a punctuation or accent on the woven cloth that brings a crinkled line to the weft

Drahomira Hampl, *Untitled* (detail), from light collection 'Loomière', 2006. Twisted lurex and cassette tape weft and transparent twisted polyester film warp, plain weave with cut weft floats, 24-shaft loom.

PHOTOGRAPHER: JIRI HAMPL

when compressed between picks, and springs out of each pick when allowed to hang free at each end. Hampl's cassette tape sample is part of a larger collection of woven textiles that are 'all transparent and have a quadrangle in the middle made from different materials, which were laid between transparent yarn during weaving'. The series includes paper yarn, a bast fibre, phosphorescent yarn and, Hampl explains, '[cassette] tape, because it looks like flat yarn, is reliable and glossy but still not commonly found in a woven textile'.

British designer **Nadia-Anne Ricketts** wondered if it would be 'possible to weave music into fabric' and found that it was a question that snowballed.[17] Originally trained as a professional dancer, Ricketts worked in the performing industry for over a decade before studying weaving at Central Saint Martin's College of Art and Design in London. She was attracted to the discipline because she 'liked the idea of learning a skill and the structure behind it. I am a logical person. There is the satisfaction of a final fabric, made from nothing'. The possibilities of Jacquard weaving, which she sees as a 'middle point between print and weave', have provided a place where she can 'incorporate the two'.

During her undergraduate studies, Ricketts saw the connection between a music file and the binary code used to control a Jacquard loom. Collaborating with the music producer and computer programmer Matt Brown allowed her to develop a software program that allows an MP3 file of anything – from a poetry reading to an instrument – to be translated into a visual format. The broken-down sound waves can map every sound frequency, rhythm and amplitude, leaving Ricketts with countless options for patterns that can then be drafted as weave structures.

Contacts in the music industry have been significant in the development of Ricketts's work. 'Friends are DJs and music producers', she says. 'People who

ABOVE LEFT: Nadia-Anne Ricketts, *Breakya (Matt Brown)* (detail), from 'BeatWoven' collection, 2009. Polyester, monofilament and metallic Lurex weft and polyester warp, Jacquard loom.
PHOTOGRAPHER: KIMBERLY HURRY

ABOVE RIGHT: Nadia-Anne Ricketts, *Lullaby* (SOS remix, The Cure – *Lullaby*) (detail), from 'BeatWoven' collection, 2009. Polyester, monofilament and metallic Lurex weft and polyester warp, Jacquard loom.
PHOTOGRAPHER: KIMBERLY HURRY

LEFT: Nadia-Anne Ricketts, *Dubcut* (Filth & Splendour, Itch records) (detail), from 'BeatWoven' collection, 2009. Nylon, polyester and metallic Lurex weft and polyester warp, Jacquard loom.
PHOTOGRAPHER: KIMBERLY HURRY

make music are a lot more interested in what I do.' Crucially, using sound files from DJs also means that she can obtain the copyright permission to use the data. Much of her collection is based on house dance music, which becomes not only the pattern of the cloth, but also directs her decisions about colour palette and fabric weight. 'I want to connect the genre of music or song to the fabric. For instance, a heavy track, very bass–y, is woven as a heavy fabric with dark colours.' 'BeatWoven' is the result: a dark, shimmery collection suggestive of the low, pulsing lights of a packed nightclub.

Eleanor Pritchard, *Marker Blanket* (ink colourway), 2011. Wool weft and warp, double-cloth block structure, Dobby loom. PHOTOGRAPHER: ELEANOR PRITCHARD

625 Line Blanket, 2010. Wool weft and warp, block and float structure, Dobby loom. PHOTOGRAPHER: ELEANOR PRITCHARD

Signal Blanket (otter colourway), 2011. Wool weft and warp, double-cloth block structure, Dobby loom. PHOTOGRAPHER: ELEANOR PRITCHARD

British designer **Eleanor Pritchard** is based in London, but production of her double-cloth blankets takes place in rural Wales at the Melin Teifi Mill in Carmarthenshire. Pritchard's collections tend to 'reference my interest in traditional weave structures; double cloth is a very old Welsh tradition'.[18] In 2010 she released two designs inspired by early television transmission systems, *405 Line*, a black and white design, and *625 Line*, a colour version. The titles refer to the number of scanning lines needed to transmit black and white and colour television, respectively. Her 2011–12 collection includes the blankets *Signal* and *Marker*, based on the visual depictions of sound waves, radio transmissions and Morse code. The patterns are graphic and clean, woven in a spare palette of white with black or dark brown, with the exception of *625 Line* and its nod to early colour television images. The work visually suggests a 'feeling of a pulse, hence the signal idea', Pritchard explains of her design references.

While many of the projects discussed in this chapter aspire to capture and translate sound – into pattern, colour or simply more sound – textiles are also celebrated for their ability to reduce sound. Fabric is often introduced into built environments to reduce noise levels. Based in the Netherlands, the Polish textile designer **Aleksandra Gaca** designs 'self-engineered and three-dimensional weaves' that provide effective acoustic properties.[19] Gaca describes her 'Architextile' collection as 'decorative, acoustic fabrics'. 'The research into the technical possibilities and application of dimensional textiles resulted in surprising combinations and contrasts – contrasts in material, matt next to shining, hard next to soft, but also contrast in content – high-tech in combination with natural materials, technical next to more traditional solutions, and cool [and] detached versus warm and inviting.'[20]

Gaca studied at the Royal Academy in The Hague and, when introduced to weaving, 'fell in love. I was fascinated with the technique when I realised you can create constructions. Every time I weave, I discover new possibilities'.[21] Structure, in particular the possibilities of three-dimensional weaving, is Gaca's primary concern and she explains that from the start she was interested in the challenge of translating her prototypes into industrial production, saying, '[It is] not only for me to have as a piece of art, I also wanted to translate [my weavings] into a product and realise them not just by hand.' The majority of her work is now produced industrially and hand finished, a balance she sees as bringing together the best of craft and design. A small 24-shaft loom in her studio is used 'only to discover constructions'. Since 2001 she has worked closely with the TextielLab at the Textiel Museum Tilburg, the Netherlands, to produce complex three-dimensional woven structures, such as the 'Architextile' collection, woven on the centre's Jacquard looms.

After her studies, Gaca worked with Ferdinand Visser at Hybrids and Fusion and began to see how her interest in weaving three-dimensional objects could be translated into three-dimensional textiles with applications in the contract market. Today, her textiles are often introduced to spaces that have acoustic problems, a solution she sees as 'a good combination of something functional and decorative', although her work also makes its way into private homes for its aesthetic appeal. Materials tend to be chosen for the contrasts in visual and tactile qualities: polyester mixed with wool, for example, or mohair and lurex. Her

BELOW: Aleksandra Gaca, *Floro* (details of front and back) 2010. Weft of cotton, wool, viscose and polyester and a cotton warp, various weave structures, Jacquard loom for Town Hall of Oss, the Netherlands.

PHOTOGRAPHER: ALEKSANDRA GACA

Aleksandra Gaca, *Selo* (detail, right), 2011, for Architextile project Crematorium, Lepenhof, Delft, the Netherlands. Cotton, wool, viscose and polyester weft and cotton warp, various structures, Jacquard loom. Colourway is the first panel in a fourteen panel installation with seven colour graduations.

PHOTOGRAPHER: STIJN KRIELE

restrained palette translates well into a variety of settings. 'When I design fabric, I always work with subtle colours. If I use colour, it can influence the structure and some combinations of colour can change my ideas about structure. So I don't use hard colours', she explains. A recent urgent commission came from a crematorium in Delft, which prior to the installation of her work had such an acoustic problem that even hushed conversations could be heard. Fourteen acoustic panels were installed in the auditorium of the crematorium and funeral centre. 'Besides the design function, noise reduction was a prerequisite – an essential requirement to help create a tranquil interior appropriate to the ceremonial function of this building.'[22]

'Making it Digital: Woven Wood' is a collaboration between the British product designer **Gary Allson** and the Greek weaver **Ismini Samanidou**. In 2008 the pair were set the challenge of using the digital as a platform and responded by combining their respective interests in weaving cloth and milling wood. The starting point for their inspiration was 13th-century oak panel walls, carved to represent folded linen, seen in the Godolphin House in Cornwall, England. Captivated by the 'idea of luxury textiles described in timber', the pair connected the use of woven tapestries hung in the past for their acoustic properties and ability to temper cold draughts, with wood panelling – which can similarly insulate against sound and climate.

Scotweave, the software Samanidou uses to create visualisations of woven cloth prior to weaving, caught Allson's eye. They requested the three-dimensional visualisation file from David Kemp, the software manufacturer, and fed – with some patient tweaking – the data from the weave file into the milling

 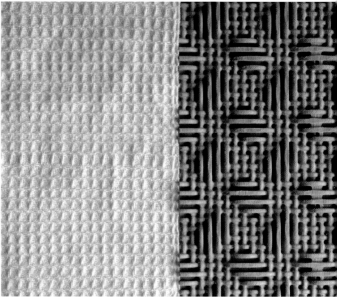

machine. Allson explains that, 'A key part of project is the relationship between different digital equipment. A Jacquard loom lives in a weaving factory and a milling machine lives in production facilities. Bringing the two together at the level of the digital means they then grow new kinds of objects.'[23] Samanidou observes, 'It is fascinating to see how different software works. Weaving software has a particular objective, which I understand, having worked with it for years. I found it very different to observe different software and watch someone else using it. I could see within the milling aspect information in an aesthetic that appealed to me: lines, planes, tool paths: things you dream to weave with!'

Initial trials to mill the wood at the scale of the textile meant that the material of the wood – the grain – overpowered the work. Magnifying the weave structure allowed the weave to become more visible. Allson describes the project as an 'attempt to explore disassociated pieces of equipment'. But by challenging the milling equipment to 'weave', Allson saw that he began to understand his familiar material of timber in a different way. Digital tools provide incredible precision, but materials such as wood are also rife with vagaries. Humidity, for example, can impact on the properties of the material dramatically. Samanidou adds that the textile too comes with its particularities, from the spin of the yarn (S- or Z-twist), to the part of the animal that the wool is originally clipped from. Anything that differs from the same manufacturing lot makes the raw materials of textile production full of variations as well. 'Those tiny differences, from the tension of the loom to different finishes, is what I love about materials', Samanidou confirms.

LEFT: Ismini Samanidou and Gary Allson, *Woven Wood: Twill Oak*, 2010. Milled on a MDX500 Roland CNC mill with a 6 mm (¼in.) ball nose.
PHOTOGRAPHER: ISMINI SAMANIDOU AND GARY ALLSON

RIGHT: Ismini Samanidou and Gary Allson, *Woven Wood: Honeycomb*, 2008. Linen warp and weft woven on an 8-shaft Harris hand loom. Oak, milled on a MDX500 Roland CNC mill with a 6 mm (¼ in.) ball nose.
PHOTOGRAPHER: MATT JESSOP

CHAPTER FIVE

Emotion

TEXTILES ENJOY A PHYSICAL INTIMACY WITH OUR BODIES because of their proximity to our skin. In addition to this, the production of textiles, particularly when undertaken by hand, is incredibly time-consuming. As a result of the time invested in the creation of woven textiles and the intimate associations we have with their materials, textiles often feel as though they are imbued with something more than the technical accomplishments of their creation. The combination of their making and use can make textiles emotionally charged, and artists take the emotional associations we have with textiles as a starting point for recording intimate and personal feelings within the woven structure. Often, these emotions are suggested rather than spoken. The results are visually powerful, but bear messages that remain open to interpretation.

The late French artist **Louise Bourgeois** lived much of her life in America and created some of her most powerful work towards the end of her career, when she returned to the materials of her troubled childhood and began creating sculptures in cloth. Bourgeois's family history has been well documented by the artist and represents a mixture of fact and fiction, stories that explain and at the same time contradict the complex emotions she articulates through her work. What can be agreed is that the artist's family ran a tapestry restoration business in France at the turn of the twentieth century.[1] Woven textiles, their unravelling and repair were a regular sight during her childhood. Bourgeois reveals that her father's affair with the woman meant to be her childhood governess left her with feelings of betrayal and grief. Her father's blatancy and her mother's seeming acceptance of the situation are referred to in her writings, drawings and sculptures.[2] Throughout much of her career in New York City, Bourgeois tackled the 'serious' materials of an artist of her generation: metal and stone were used to create large-scale permanent sculptures such as her well-known series of spiders, which she likened to the maternal figure. But in the final decades of her life, the textile made an increasing appearance in smaller-scale works and critics have observed that these works are to be some of the most moving of her career.

OPPOSITE: Louise Bourgeois, *Untitled*, 2002. Tapestry and aluminium, 43.1 x 30.4 x 30.4 cm (17 x 12 x 12 in.).

PHOTOGRAPHER: CHRISTOPHER BURKE © LOUISE BOURGEOIS TRUST

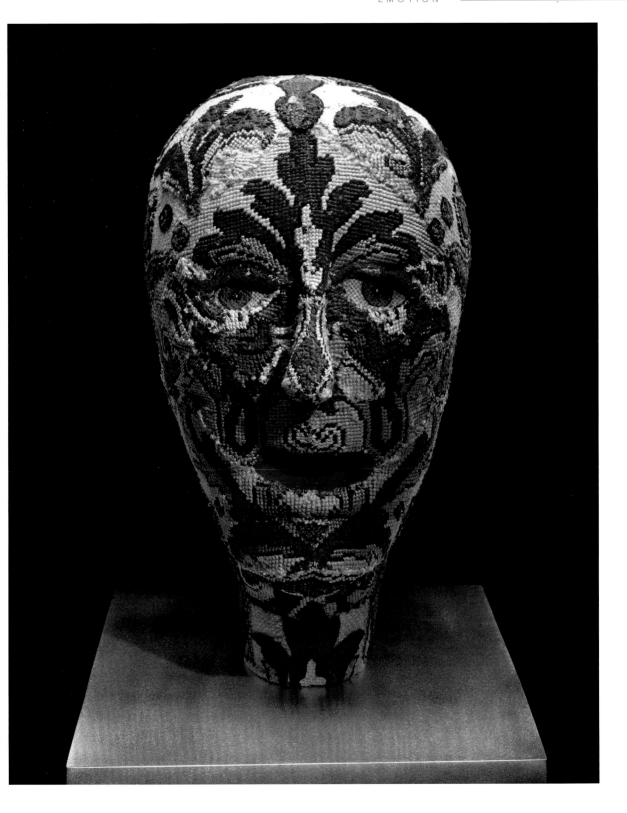

Ane Henrikesen, *Trembling 1*, 2005. Bed cloth weft and silk and viscose sizing warp, tapestry weaving, 2.4 x 3.2 m (7 ft 11 in. x 10 ft 6 in.).

PHOTOGRAPHER: ANDERS SUNE BERG

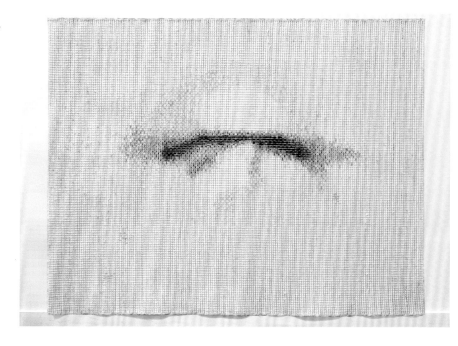

Bourgeois did not weave, but her familiarity with the repair of woven cloth seems to have provided her with a disarming sensitivity for the power of weaving and stitching to convey emotion. The late Rozsika Parker, in her introduction to the second edition of *The Subversive Stitch*, published in 2010, writes that: '[Bourgeois's] work with fabric is associated directly with female sexuality, the unconscious and the body. Familiar with psychoanalysis, she explores the infantile roots of female sexuality in the family through her own history, which was closely tied to textiles, as her parents ran a tapestry restoration business … Particularly powerful are her recent fabric heads. Taking the template of the portrait bust in stone or bronze, Louise Bourgeois reworks the form in patched-together fabric: tapestry, towelling, ticking or pink bandages. The medium of personal life well conveys internal conflict, age, pain and doubt.'[3]

'My pictures are, in a sense, like my skin – an expression of something vulnerable', states the Danish tapestry artist **Ane Henriksen**.[4] Henriksen weaves massive abstract tapestries. 'I try to contain the world around me and transform it to fit my reality – to a new kind of internal logic, a stillness.' The emotional power of Henriksen's work, like that of Bourgeois, often suggests an unsettling mixture of emotions. She describes her work as 'repulsive yet appealing – aesthetics on the threshold of pain – searching with a mixture of doubt and conviction'.[5] In the 'Trembling' series, woven with flesh tones in 2005, a mouth-like shape is centred in the middle of each large work in the three-piece series. This central abstract shape is crimson – a little like the colour of pain suggesting an injury or wound that may be under repair.

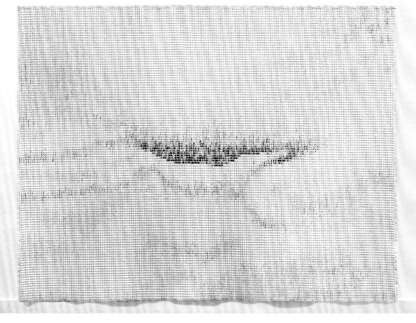

Ane Henrikesen, *Trembling 2*, 2005. Bed cloth weft and silk and viscose sizing warp, tapestry weaving, 2.4 x 3.2 m (7 ft 11 in. x 10 ft 6 in.).

PHOTOGRAPHER: ANDERS SUNE BERG

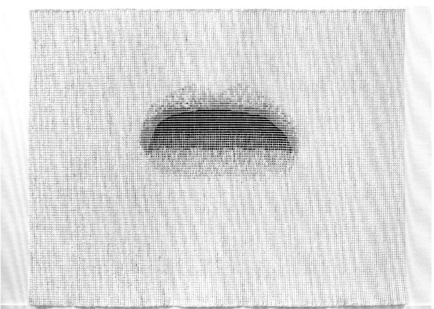

Viewed closely, the weft of each tapestry is comprised of numerous colours and textures: cut strips of old bedclothes in various shades of pink, thin sewing threads and fat strips of fabric once belonging to a quilt all pack down into a single pick. Peer even closer and single threads of bright green, yellow and orange can be found buried deep in the weave. The odd worn, fabric-covered button can even be spotted. Jette Hartvig refers to these buttons as 'little

Ane Henrikesen, *Trembling 3*, 2005. (detail above) Bed cloth weft and silk and viscose sizing warp, tapestry weaving, 2.4 x 3.2 cm (7 ft 11 in. x 10 ft 6 in.).

PHOTOGRAPHER: ANDERS SUNE BERG

stowaways' and mentions that 'At one time, they were painstakingly sewn into the fabric of the quilt, which was then cut into pieces and recycled ... they turn up here and there and tell, almost like a Hans Christian Andersen fairy tale, about their past as buttons and about their new found and important significance as messengers.'[6] The buttons here are no longer functional, their buttonholes long squashed closed and hidden elsewhere in the tapestry, but their presence reminds us that cloth can have many lives and bear witness to many events.

In moments of extreme emotion, spoken and written language often fail us, frequently doing no better than offering up tired clichés. And then there are experiences that, even when shared, simply refuse to sit within the logic and order that language imposes. Louise Mazanti observes of Henriksen's work, 'We are getting in around behind language's conventional thinking and thereby behind the intellectual and thought-related repartees that ordinarily enable us to distance ourselves from life's deeper layers.'[7] Mazanti feels the messy, unsanctioned emotions of discomfort, as well as the marvel, that Henriksen's tapestries capture – emotions that are not fun to feel or even possible to explain. But Henriksen confronts them nonetheless. 'With emotion-bearing threads, I want to form a space, and the possibility of escape', she asserts. 'I do not try to distract the viewer's attention, but to call them to attention – and perhaps awaken them to wonder.'[8]

British artist **Shane Waltener** often works with participatory projects, involving the public in the production of large-scale knit and crochet structures. 'There is no exact plan as to how the pieces are made. A lot of the decision-making lies with the participants contributing to the making of the piece', he reveals of these organic creations.[9] In 2008, a commission by Compton Verney, England for 'The Fabric of Myth' exhibition encouraged Waltener to respond to the Greek myth of Penelope, famous for undoing her weaving to stall unwanted suitors. *Destiny* is a far more structured work than Waltener's typical output, and is based on a tension between control and chance.

Penelope's story is essentially one of loyalty. She wove by day, but unpicked her work by night while she waited for news of her husband's return. Historians often suggest that she may have been weaving a funerary shroud, but the historian Elizabeth Wayland Barber is not convinced that the unpicking of a simple woven structure would have gone unnoticed by a community familiar with the rhythms of weaving. Instead, she suggests that Penelope must have woven a pictorial tapestry – something slow to weave – that would have allowed her surreptitious unpicking to have been less noticeable to those around her. 'Homer's audience', Barber writes, 'would have known that only the weaving of a non-repetitive pattern such as a story is so very time-consuming, but we who no longer weave or regularly watch others weave are more easily misled.'[10] Kathryn Sullivan Kruger also suggests Penelope wove and unpicked a more

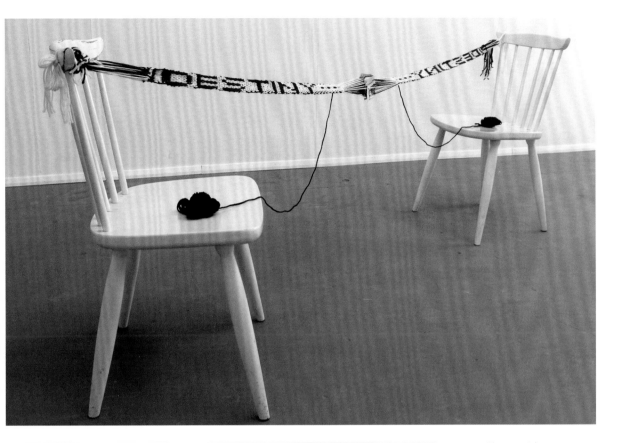

ABOVE: Shane Waltener,
Destiny, 2008. Tablet
weaving with wool yarn,
playing cards and chairs.
Installed at Compton Verney,
England.

PHOTOGRAPHER: SHANE WALTENER

LEFT: Shane Waltener, *Destiny*
(detail), 2008. Tablet weaving
with wool yarn, playing
cards and chairs. Installed at
Compton Verney, England.

PHOTOGRAPHER: SHANE WALTENER

complex cloth, although she attributes the oversight of the nightly undoing of the weaving slightly differently. 'Although Homer never describes the pattern on Laertes' shroud, Penelope must have been weaving a storytelling cloth. A simple winding cloth could have been completed in a matter of weeks and would not have been complex enough to deceive the suitors for almost four years. Every day she weaves an intricate pattern complementing the high station of her father-in-law and every night, once her servants and suitors have fallen asleep, she picks out the pattern and unravels most of the threads she has woven that day. Since the intricacies of cloth-making did not concern men in this society, they were easily duped.'[11]

Using tablet weaving, Waltener's *Destiny* addresses narrative and myth in textiles. He explains, 'I had the idea of two people weaving facing each other, playing a game as it were, as the weaving is done. Playing a game and the use of playing cards, a weaving ritual of some kind, determines a set of manoeuvres. The planned pattern and also the accidental pattern are created because the reverse is woven on the opposite side. Agreement is reached between the two weavers to complete the pattern.' Waltener's negotiated construction is a model of give and take, action and consequence that runs through all of our emotional lives. He elaborates: 'The sequence of actions, or the playing of the cards, results in the weaving of the word "destiny". It is a repeatable sequence of actions, a physical incantation formulated within the traditions of this ancient craft and performed between two people. The resulting woven pieces mirror each other and the reading of the words leads the eye to the set of cards. Chance here appears thus to be predetermined.' Ironically, to communicate the woven text, Waltener found he had to control chance: 'With the *Destiny* piece, as the words have to be read, less is left to chance, contrary to what the playing cards might suggest. The "fate" of the piece is in effect sealed in advance of it being created.' Some might say many of our relationships are the result of a similar mixture of intention and luck.

Dutch artist and designer **Jeroen Vinken** has a practice that spans the worlds of commercial design and art. His engagement with Jacquard weaving began in 1999 with the support of the Textiel Museum Tilburg, the Netherlands and TextielLab, which houses specialist textile equipment that artists and designers throughout Europe regularly access to realise large-scale textile work. The centre provides various disciplines with the opportunity to work and aims to stimulate interest in textile techniques. In addition to this, designers and the textile industry are given the opportunity to develop experimental projects that may later translate into industrial production. Vinken was the first artist to develop a new woven collection on the centre's Jacquard looms and comments that his interests lie in 'developing things that do not exist yet'.[12] In his commercial design work, a new series of Jacquard-woven curtain fabrics entitled 'Mazzo' have recently been developed under the company name Henskin. Imagery is

Jeroen Vinken, *Mazzo Modesto* (detail left), 2009. Polyester weft and warp, digital Jacquard loom, of 1.5 m (5 ft) wide and length of design repeat approx. 36 m (39 yd) long.

PHOTOGRAPHER: JEROEN VINKEN

LEFT: Jeroen Vinken, *Incanto 4*, 2010. Polyester weft and cotton warp, digital Jacquard, approx. 215 x 155 cm (7 x 5 ft).

PHOTOGRAPHER: JEROEN VINKEN

RIGHT: Jeroen Vinken, *Exercise 8*, 2008. Polyester weft and cotton warp, digital Jacquard, approx. 210 x 155 cm (6 ft 10 in. x 5 ft).

PHOTOGRAPHER: JEROEN VINKEN

based on a bouquet altered in a photo editor by layering, blurring, stretching and pixellating the original design. The collection's colourways are the result of variations in saturation and lightness of the design's three basic hues of red, green and blue. The repeat varies from 36–96 m (118–315 ft) and means that every curtain cut to order is essentially bespoke as it captures a different portion of the enormous repeat.

Throughout Vinken's work, the 'possibilities of photorealism' often appear by way of visual juxtapositions based on photographic collages. While 'Mazzo' challenges the technical limitations of designing a repeat pattern for industry, his artistic practice explores more intimate themes. The floral motif is perhaps the most ubiquitous and familiar pattern for textile design, but Vinken unsettles this familiarity by creating what he describes as 'bouquets with human limbs'.[13] These works are part of an ongoing series named 'Incanto', Italian for 'enchantment'. The imagery is surprising: body parts are intertwined with plants, suggestive of a latent fertility present in all living things. Vinken clarifies: 'What fascinates me is … on the one hand a "soul" being present in all living things, but at the same time something of impotence and hopelessness … a "love in vain" perhaps.'[14]

The unexpected combinations can make the viewer feel like something of a voyeur, encouraged to stare but not convinced that their interpretation should be admitted to others. As Brigitte de Swart observes, 'Running through Jeroen's oeuvre is an association with the erotic … Layer by layer they peel away the raw illusions of the soul and blur limitations and traditional values.'[15] Vinken is reluctant to explain the imagery, but confirms, 'The "meeting" of different elements fascinates me',[16] 'this tension between the masculine and feminine, tenderness and hardness, vulnerability and power'.[17]

Protection is the recurring theme of recent work by Australian **Liz Williamson**. Her 'Loop' series from 2007 and 2008 of woven cotton and leather adorns the body as a necklace might do, but also suggests something of a talisman. In previous work, Williamson has considered the role of darning in textile repair. She describes her aims for the series as twofold. The first part continues her exploration of protection through darning, now shifted to consider 'creating a protective container or shape [that] could hold or cover and surround the body'. The second consideration was to make 'a wearable object more aligned to jewellery; not a scarf, but dressing the neck with something aligned to a neck-piece'.[18]

'I tested a whole series of yarns', Williamson remembers of the series' evolution. 'I had leather in the studio – it didn't work to weave [the leather] consecutively as weft – but inserting it into the shed and looping it over the cloth to form loops worked as a cover.' The leather helps provide the rounded shape of each piece, which is woven in 1.5 m (5 ft) strips and then stitched into tubes. According to Gary Sangster, '[Williamson's work is] seductive in form and seductive to the eye. Seductive but not necessarily erotic. These works, capable of both sexualising and referencing the body, are not really triggers for desire in the way representations of the body can be. They mark entirely different territory, activating a semiotic function that reflects memory and identity.'[19] 'I do see it as bodily protection', Williamson offers as analysis of her own work. '[It is] not about protecting our borders – a big issue in Australia. I am against a lot of the efforts to keep out refugees. [Instead] it is about the body. But what body or what kind of body is open to interpretation.'

In 2009 and 2010, British artist **Lucy Brown** created the woven

Liz Williamson, *Loop* from the 'Protection' series, 2008. Cotton and leather weft and cotton warp, hand-woven plain weave with supplementary weft on eight-shaft Glimakra countermarch loom.

PHOTOGRAPHER: IAN HOBBS

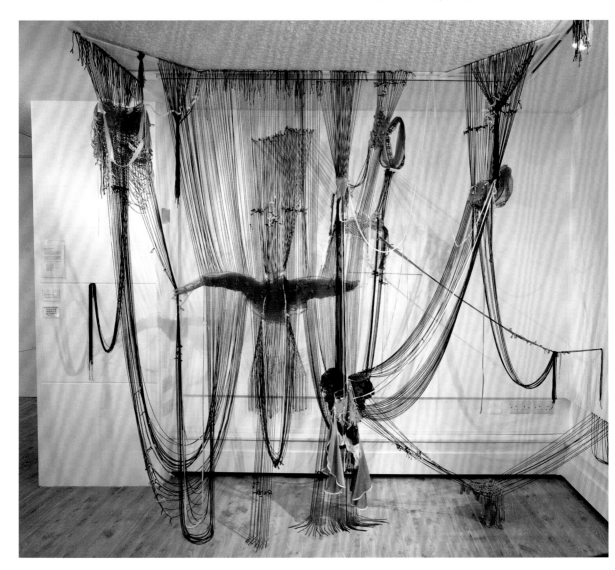

installation *I Lost Myself Because I Thought I Wanted to Be With You Forever…* at the Rochester Art Gallery in England. Funded by the Theo Moorman Trust for Weavers, the work was woven in Brown's studio, followed by freehand techniques during installation where warps were extended and individual warp threads pinned to the ceiling, wall or floor. 'A small amount of weaving takes place in situ, meaning that the form of the installation will change each time it is shown', Brown states.[20] The work was woven with a brown rayon upholstery cord warp, using weft materials that included a cotton velvet Laura Ashley dress and Marks & Spencer's 1970s negligées and lingerie. As well as being attracted to the simplicity and history of weaving, Brown explains that '[The technique] allows me to keep the integrity of the selected garments. Some of the clothes which I use are also woven, so the idea of weaving with already woven cloth feeds into the woven narratives of re-making, re-weaving, re-constructing.' The emotionally charged titles of her work are determined only after completion of the installation and referred to, until then, by the equally evocative working title 'Limbo'. Each title is drawn from notes and thoughts she jots down either while weaving the garments that make up the weft or when wearing the garments prior to weaving.[21]

Brown adopts a two-step creation system that brings together two distinctly different working methods. 'These woven offerings develop over two stages', she volunteers. 'The first stage is making; weaving on the loom and will normally take place in the privacy of the studio space. The second stage is when works are taken to an exhibition space and are extended, suspended and re-tensioned.'[22] The majority of the weaving takes place in her studio, followed, for her Rochester Art Gallery exhibition, by a further 15 days in total devoted to the installation: five before the opening of the show and a further ten after the opening. She describes her weaving time in the studio as an 'immersive way of working that is intense and intimate'. 'The work comes from within. In the studio it is a very personal, one-to-one dialogue. In the gallery space the work grows and takes up its own space. I see it like an opening-out, an expansion.'[23]

Brown's chosen materials are sourced from second-hand and charity

OPPOSITE AND RIGHT:
Lucy Brown, *I Lost Myself Because I Thought I Wanted to Be With You Forever…* , 2009–10. Warp of rayon upholstery cord, weft of vintage and second-hand garments including cotton velvet Laura Ashley dress and Marks & Spencer's 1970s negligées and lingerie. Hand woven on an upright Egar loom, 2.5 x 3.5 x 1 m (8 ft 2 in. x 11 ft 6 in. x 3 ft 3 in.), installed at Rochester Art Gallery, England.

PHOTOGRAPHER: DAVID RAMKALAWON

shops, as well as pieces from her own life-long interest in collecting clothing, and they are often worn by her prior to being used for weaving. Catherine Harper observes that '[She] uses the discarded clothing of the old – vintage undergarments, slips and petticoats, intimate materials in colours called "rose" or "mint" or even "flesh" … [and is] self-confessedly interested in the edges, the boundaries of the weave and of the clothing. Labels and stitched seams get reconfigured in her works and demonstrate the body selvedges …'[24] These details are largely unplanned, a moment Brown likens to being 'a bit like stepping into a black hole: you don't know what is going to happen'. Once cut from the loom, Brown continues the weaving process using freehand techniques she has developed and 'physical, sensory, emotional and psychological engagement with selected clothing'. 'The speculative play around the visible and invisible history of the raw material and the internal and external surfaces all contribute to these responses … There are themes around the unfinished and unresolved, meaning the works are in a constant state of "becoming".'[25]

Bahamian artist **Janine Antoni**'s *Views of Slumber*, first performed in 1993, involved the artist sleeping in a gallery attached to electroencephalography equipment (commonly known as an EEG) that records the eye movements of the REM sleep phase. This data was then translated into a pattern that the artist wove by hand in the gallery each day. Glenn Adamson writes of the work, '"Slumber" combines an insistent narcissism (or, at least, self-fascination) with an undercutting of stable identity. Are her dreams, her deepest desires, really mapped in those zigzag lines?'[26] On the one hand, the intimate record of her dreams is exposed for all to see – woven each day into the scroll of cloth. But in another way, these private experiences remain entirely private, coded in a form that cannot be read by viewers. More tangible than the actual stuff of her dreams is the awareness of time that runs throughout the installation. Night and sleep, our 'lost' hours, are physically mapped as the warp suspended above her bed grows into the blanket she sleeps beneath.

More recently, the American weaver **Lia Cook** has collaborated with neuroscientists on a series of Jacquard weavings that map brain activity when viewing textiles. Rather than investigating the abstract realm of the dream, Cook is exploring how the brain responds to portraits woven into cloth compared to their photographic equivalent. In experiments, the same portrait in woven and photographic versions is shown to subjects and their brain activity monitored with an EEG, EMG (electromyography) and fMRI (functional magnetic resonance imaging). The empirical data of these experiments confirms our familiar, albeit intuitive, understanding of textiles: even when the photograph and the weaving are optically similar because of viewing distance, the weaving triggers emotional responses in the viewer's brain that the photograph does not.

Cook has long worked with Jacquard-woven portraits and childhood

ABOVE: Janine Antoni,
Slumber, 1993–2000.
COURTESY OF THE ARTIST AND LUHRING
AUGUSTINE, NEW YORK

LEFT: Janine Antoni weaving
Slumber, 1993–2000.
COURTESY OF THE ARTIST AND LUHRING
AUGUSTINE, NEW YORK

photographs of herself have been a source of imagery. The 'Su' series, for example, uses an image of Cook as a child but with variations in the woven construction of the image. She explains that '[The work] lends itself to multiple interpretations. When people look at the series they see different emotional expressions depending on how it is translated.'[27] More recently, these variations have included the portrait overlaid with strands of brain connectivity that look eerily similar to threads. In other weavings, the subject is shown wearing the EEG equipment, while viewing a weaving by Cook or reaching out to touch the weaving in an effort to confirm what he or she is seeing.

'I sometimes say that this is not art, it is science', Cook jokes of the practical demands of working collaboratively with neuroscientists and learning some of the functions of the complex software used to map the brain. 'I am still learning a lot about the Track Vis software. It is science software so there is a learning curve. You can isolate paths in the brain and I can become much more specific about what I am using and what it means', she explains. The research is a departure from the work that Cook has created for a number of years, both in terms of process and content. 'Before the series, I worked in a much more individual way. It is popular now for people to work collaboratively, but in my case in the past I have always worked more individually and liked my own private space and process. Right now this [collaboration] is appealing to me – maybe because I have already done a lot of individual work – and the interactive process is exciting to the scientists.' Instead of weaving the nuances in the emotional reading of her own face, Cook is now making weavings of weavings, mapping in the brain the response of others as they observe her woven image.

TOP: Lia Cook, *Tracts Remind*, 2011. Cotton and rayon weft and cotton warp, hand-woven Jacquard, 172.7 x 132.1 cm (68 x 52 in.) (detail shown on right).

PHOTOGRAPHER: LIA COOK

BOTTOM: Lia Cook, *Facing Touch*, 2011. Cotton and rayon weft and cotton warp, hand-woven Jacquard, 137.2 x 129.5 cm (54 x 51 in.) (detail shown on right). Inspired by neuroscience collaboration University of Pittsburgh TREND Project, USA.

PHOTOGRAPHER: LIA COOK

CHAPTER SIX

Community

THE CREATION AND USE OF WOVEN TEXTILES CAN BRING US TOGETHER. It can offer a system of thinking, as well as a way of making. Woven textiles appear in the shared public spaces of museums, trains and hotel lobbies, as well as less expected locations such as construction sites. Designers with sustainable agendas are weaving with the community in mind, working to reduce the waste that the textile industry is, regrettably, notorious for producing. Recycled weft *and* warp materials from a surprising range of sources are making an appearance in woven textiles. Artists also approach weaving as a group endeavour and bring communities together to share and learn skills. These events promote much needed conversations about the place of textile manufacturing today and the impact of its rapid departure from what were once thriving production centres of Europe and North America. It is in these conversations that communities – and individuals – can begin to determine our responsibilities for the future.

Swedish artist **Petter Hellsing** trained as a sculptor and arrived at weaving via an interest in computerised embroidery. A commission at a hospital in Gothenburg launched his beginnings with Jacquard weaving, which by his own admission progressed thanks to a fair bit of trial and error followed by a grant from the Swedish government to study at the Montreal Centre for Contemporary Textiles in Canada. 'Most people working with Jacquard have a weave background,' Hellsing observes, 'and most use it traditionally. I'm coming from a sculpture background. I weave the cloth and then I start working with it, mixing it together.'[1]

In 2010, the National Public Art Council of Sweden commissioned Hellsing to create *Contemporary Patterns* for the Aircraft Museum in Linköping, Sweden. Installation of the woven black and white stage curtain marked the museum's reopening and a new emphasis within their exhibits on the broader implications of history. Hellsing's unconventional approach to weaving explains why the curtain is cut and then 'sewn together as a patchwork. This was an opportunity to see what has happened with cloth and treat it like collage'. Exhibits about the machinery of the Cold War era had once been the museum's focus, but as Hellsing explains, 'I wanted my piece to continue the story after the

Cold War … I was brought up with the idea that Sweden was neutral during the war; that we had clean hands because that was the official story. There is now discussion of the Swedish role during the Second World War, but it has come very late.' The commission also provided Hellsing with an opportunity to reflect on history: 'I have chosen historical events that are, so to say, "in the air" now with [images of] people that are symbols for what we think today are turning points in history. The curtain is a segment of time that will age … People in the future will face other challenges and see incidents and contexts that are hidden from us today.'[2]

Petter Hellsing, *Contemporary Patterns*, 2010. Cotton weft and warp, pieced digital Jacquard weave, 14 x 6.5 m (15 x 7 yd). Aircraft Museum, Linköping, Sweden.

PHOTOGRAPHER: PETRA HELLBERG

Petter Hellsing,
Contemporary Patterns
(detail), 2010. Cotton weft
and warp, pieced digital
Jacquard weave. Aircraft
Museum, Linköping,
Sweden.

PHOTOGRAPHER: PETRA HELLBERG

Images for the Jacquard weaving were sourced from the internet at the time of the commission. Image quality was not a priority, although the ability of weaving to capture imagery 'in the material – not on the surface' offered an important distinction for Hellsing. Woven in five shades of grey, the low-resolution pictures allude to the transitory nature of news headlines that are front-page one day and forgotten the next. Photoshop was used to combine the news images and add over-scale traditional weave patterns. The introduction of visual patterns to the imagery is intended to suggest that history itself is yet another (ever changing) pattern. Revealing his scepticism for 'official' history, but also speaking of history on a personal level, Hellsing volunteers, 'If the pattern does not fit you have to change the pattern and if the history does not fit, you have to change history. Patterns are the knowledge you have today, but when a situation changes like economics and politics, then the map has been rewritten.' Hellsing's collaged map of recent headlines reminds us that versions of history, both the personal and the national, are always multiple.

Norwegian artist **Runa Carlsen** installed *The New Hotspot* on the scaffolding of a construction site in the Bjørvika area of Oslo in 2009. She describes the work as a response to the 'rapid architectonic transformation and property development that is going on at the seaside area of Bjørvika'.[3] Carlsen worked with weaving because her chosen materials – the plastic fencing and netting that are often used to create temporary barriers during construction work – are associated with her installation site. The orange material, typically used as a barrier to block people out, here acts as a sort of loom, through which Carlsen interlaced blue netting 'weft' to create a purple fabric when viewed from a distance.

The installation was inspired by her walks back and forth between her job at the Oslo Opera House and her studio, a journey that made her more aware of the urban changes around her. Carlsen comments, 'Both the plastic fencing and netting is made of polyethylene and is based on raw oil, and is one reason why I think it had relevance as a building material in this piece. For me, this

Runa Carlsen, *The New Hotspot,* 2009. Photograph of hand-woven polyethylene construction fencing installed on scaffolding in a construction site at Bjørvika, Oslo, Norway and later exhibited at the Soft Gallery, Oslo.

PHOTOGRAPHER: ESPEN TOLLEFSEN

Runa Carlsen, *The New Hotspot*, 2009. Hand-woven polyethylene construction fencing installed on scaffolding in a construction site at Bjørvika, Oslo, Norway and later exhibited at the Soft Gallery, Oslo.

PHOTOGRAPHER: ARE CARLSEN

links it to the building project in Bjørvika that is initiated and financed by the enormous economic growth that we have built up in Norway in a short period of time. Based on chance, we discovered rich oil reserves in the North Sea in the late 1960s and the beginning of the 1970s. Basically, we are a new rich nation.'[4]

Fortuitously, the contractor, Betonmast, took up offices in the same building as Carlsen's studio and supported her request to use their scaffolding as a temporary installation site. Large-scale work has always been an interest and the contractor's prompt, positive response required her 'to find something that went quickly – a material to work with fast – I am not lazy, but my priority is not small pieces'. Remarkably, the company then used their crane to allow photography of the installation to record the area in a moment of great change. Carlsen explains that the new skyscrapers located on the far side of the bridge are nicknamed 'Accountancy Row' because 'Accountancy firms and banks are [now] the only ones who can afford to have their main offices in Bjørvika.'[5]

During the winter weeks of the installation, the work 'melted into the environment' and to a certain extent 'belonged to the construction site'. Her chosen materials are bright, but also expected in the location. It is the photographic record and the questions it poses about the gentrification of urban centres that many more have viewed. The title of the work expands the implications further, alluding not only to property development but also to our reliance on the web of wireless signals – hotspots – picked up by our computers and phones to access the internet. *The New Hotspot* speaks not only of our changing physical patterns of movement as urban landscapes change, but also of our changing patterns of movement directed by our connection to the World Wide Web. The web's giant virtual network of data increasingly directs our physical movement, determining that we stop at a certain location to send an e-mail or curtail a journey to avoid losing signal contact – keeping us connected to a giant network of virtual information by establishing invisible information routes.

Bundled up against the cold Norwegian winter, it may be excusable to overlook a weaving – however remarkable – unexpectedly installed on the scaffolding of a construction site. But there are also numerous examples of woven design closer to the ground that can pass by unnoticed in the rush of our daily lives. The British design duo **Wallace & Sewell** are known for their richly coloured woven textiles for interiors and accessories. Recently, the pair won an open competition to design a new 'moquette' fabric for the London Underground network. The London Underground remains unusual in its continued use of woven textiles, rather than plastic or metal seating.[6] Moquette is a type of durable woven fabric with a dense pile that has been used as upholstery on the underground since 1936. Wallace & Sewell's design has been named the *Barman* pattern, after Christian Barman, who oversaw the first commissioning of moquette fabric for the Tube. The design will gradually replace the existing moquettes, appearing first on refurbished Central Line trains in 2011.

'The design came about when we sat down and thought about London and iconic images', Emma Sewell explains. 'I began to sketch buildings in London from memory and experimented with how to turn these into simple shapes

ABOVE: Wallace & Sewell, *Barman* moquette, 2010. Preliminary artwork on paper. PHOTOGRAPHER: EMMA SEWELL

LEFT: Wallace & Sewell, *Barman* moquette, 2010. COURTESY OF LONDON UNDERGROUND, © TRANSPORT FOR LONDON VISUAL IMAGE SERVICES

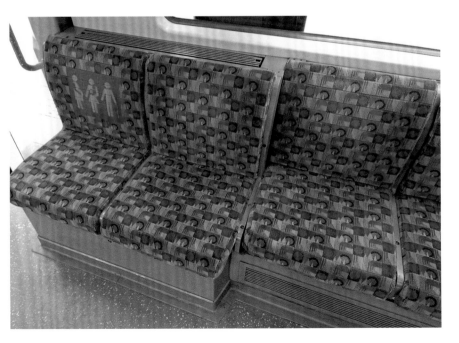

such as triangles and circles. I then played with putting the shapes together. For instance, the spire of St Paul's Cathedral is the upright inside the London Eye.'[7] Sewell studied printed as well as woven textiles and describes her influences as coming from the pared down geometric shapes of printed constructivist textiles, and the idea of camouflage to disguise a repeating pattern. The latter was a particular consideration for the commission, because of specifications that set a very small repeat for the upholstery fabric.

The commission looks to be a huge departure from Wallace & Sewell's familiar aesthetic of jewel colours and contrasting textures. Sewell agrees, but describes the opportunity as a 'refreshing challenge'. 'This is the third big project we have worked on for the organisation Transport for London. The first was a new moquette for seating on the Overground, followed by a commission for the Tramlink. In each, the specification of the fabric was set. We provided the pattern design and increasingly oversee the sampling.' Unlike much of their work, these projects are rife with design restrictions. 'It is not an endless palette of colours from the project brief; in fact it is just four colours that we had to balance in the design.' Sewell reflects that the commissions have acted as an 'interesting flip side to the work that we do'. 'Our general work is flamboyant and bespoke in a way. Designing to a tight specification is a great contrast.' Unlike the niche market the majority of their design work enjoys, the audience for moquette is huge and essentially democratic: the population of London's Tube users.

Wallace & Sewell, wool and cashmere wrap (detail), 2010. Wool, cashmere and mohair wefts and wool warp, mock leno weave, Dobby power loom.

PHOTOGRAPHER: KATE WALSH

Wallace & Sewell, silk and cashmere scarves (detail), 2011. Silk and cashmere weft and silk warp, satin weaves, Dobby power loom.

PHOTOGRAPHER: KATE WALSH

ABOVE: Ptolemy Mann, King's
Mill Hospital, England,
façade visualisations, 2006.

IMAGE COURTESY OF PTOLEMY MANN AND
SWANKE HAYDEN CONNELL ARCHITECTS

BELOW: Ptolemy Mann,
unwoven warp threads,
2006.

PHOTOGRAPHER: PTOLEMY MANN

London-based American designer **Ptolemy Mann** is another example of an established weaver whose design skills are applied beyond her trademark hand-woven textiles. Mann is well known for her hand-weavings that explore the graduated colour of ikat. But her knowledge of structure and colour extends far beyond woven cloth into projects such as the 'Adras' furnishing fabric, a collection of digital prints on linen designed by Mann for Christopher Farr Cloth and, most recently, a bespoke ikat design printed on wood for the Ercol Armoire with John Lewis. In addition to projects that translate the woven textile into printed pattern, Mann works as a colour consultant, bringing knowledge learned through weaving to the colour plans for entire buildings. She works with both internal and external colour schemes for domestic spaces as well as corporate and public projects and explains that her approach to 'spatial colour application [is] from an intuitive and logical perspective'.[8] 'With an emphasis on external architectural façades, Mann researches and produces relevant, articulate colour schemes for any type of building; using colour application through a diverse range of materials to give a scheme identity and context within its surroundings, often aiding a successful planning application.'[9]

From 2006–10 Mann worked with Swanke Hayden Connell Architects to create a system of internal and external way-finding for patients and visitors based on colour analogies for the King's Mill Hospital in Mansfield, England. In 2010, Mann worked on St Thomas's Hospital in London. Here, rather than work with a new building, Mann was invited to modify an existing exterior in what she describes as a project to 'wrap the building with a woven façade'. While this range of projects may seem to fall far beyond a weaver's knowledge, Mann chimes with Wallace & Sewell when she observes, 'Weavers are familiar working with restrictions. There are always a certain number of shafts and a certain number of opportunities to consider', likening the restrictions of the loom to design skills that can be applied to a world of design challenges.[10]

Ptolemy Mann, St Thomas
Hospital, England, façade
options, 2010.

MissoniHome, *Chevron,* 2011.

IMAGE COURTESY OF HOTEL MISSONI, EDINBURGH

The Italian knitwear company Missoni is celebrated for its use of knit fabric. The **Hotel Missoni** in Edinburgh provides something of a departure, with male staff kitted out in Missoni kilts of woven cloth. 'In October 2009, at the Opening Party of Hotel Missoni, Edinburgh, Gordon McKinnon, former vice president of Rezidor and Hotel Missoni, made a surprise appearance wearing a kilt made with the MissoniHome fabric covering the large bar sofa. I found this so impressive and so Scottishly Missoni that I decided to use it as uniform for the doormen', Rosita Missoni reveals.[11] The bold stripe pattern acknowledges the Scottish tradition of tartan cloth but in keeping with the function of tartan to communicate family ties, Missoni drew on its own extensive archive of knit patterns to develop the woven cloth. 'In our world of patterns, checks and tartans have always been there besides zigzags, stripes, dots and more fancy patterns. For the MissoniHome collections and especially for home furnishing, we translate our knitted patterns into woven ones.'

The British designers Karen Spurgin and Emma D'Arcey launched **ao for Gainsborough** in 2010 and use waste weft and warp yarn in the production of their woven textile collection. In partnership with Gainsborough silk weavers, ao have 'created a contemporary range of Jacquard woven fabric that uses naturally dyed and recycled silk and cotton yarns'.[12] Working with Gainsborough, the industrial weaving mill in Suffolk, England, the collection makes use of the waste weft and warp yarn that is planned as a buffer for each production run

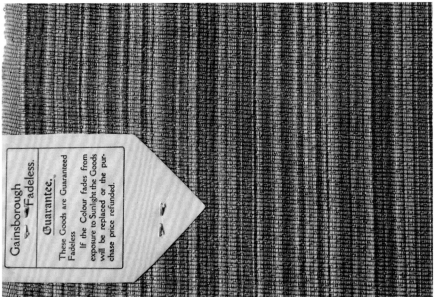

ABOVE AND LEFT: ao for Gainsborough, *WW II Stripe*, 2010. Weft and warp of silk and cotton waste warp yarn, Jacquard woven. (Image left courtesy of Gainsborough archive.)

PHOTOGRAPHER, IMAGE ABOVE: JULIET SHEATH; PHOTOGRAPHER, IMAGE LEFT: AISLING MITCHELL

to protect against any unforeseen production glitches. The Jacquard collection currently includes three designs: a floral *Flower* based on a Gainsborough archive pattern, using recycled warp composed of a melange of dark blue waste yarn; *Mineral*, inspired by marbling, which makes use of the same warp as *Flower*; and *WW II Stripe*, based on a 'recycled fabric produced by the mill during World War II when rationing required use of recycled yarn'.[13] Spurgin explains, of *WW II Stripe*, 'We had been looking to weave a stripe for our collection and this seemed perfect. The weft uses a combination of recycled post-production archive waste yarn plus some naturally dyed "leftovers". We wanted to see how natural colours combine with synthetic dyed colour.' This is one example of a modest initiative that is beginning to tackle the enormous problem of post-production waste, while keeping manufacturing based in the UK.

NUNO Corporation, *Silkworm Tray* (detail), from 'Kibiso' series, 2008. Kibiso weft material and raw silk warp, hand-woven double-sided sateen on Dobby loom. Woven by Matsuoka Kigyo Inc. and produced by the Tsuruoka Fabric Industry Cooperative.

PHOTOGRAPHER: SUE MCNAB

The Japanese company **NUNO**, led by Reiko Sudo, has long been celebrated for its innovative approach to woven textile design, which often blends high-tech and low-tech approaches. In previous work, NUNO has taken 'a special process used in the automotive industry to "chrome" door handles',[14] paused 'computer-driven looms … over and over again, row after row, so that feathers can be hand-positioned'[15] and used water-soluble backing to stitch their collection offcuts into a new, lace-like screening fabric.[16] Their recent 'Kibiso' series uses fibres spun from the hard, outermost shell of the silk cocoon, which protects the silk beneath and is normally discarded as manufacturing waste.[17] The collection was included in the 2009 Cooper-Hewitt Museum's National Design Triennial in New York City, 'Why Design Now?', because of the material and social contribution of the design. Along with finding a use for what was considered a waste product of silk production, 'Nuno also created an important social network for retired silk weavers, who are responsible for hand-weaving the kibiso textiles in Tsuruoka, in northern Japan. Many of these women have spent their entire lives working with silkworms and possess invaluable knowledge of silk manufacturing. In order to make yarn out of the very gelatinous kibiso fibre, the weavers split the fibre by hand into a yarn, which is then machine-loomed.'[18]

NUNO Corporation, *Kibiso Stripe* (detail), from 'Kibiso' series, 2008. Spun silk and kibiso weft and raw silk warp, hand-woven plain weave on four-shaft loom. Woven by the Tsuruoka hand-weavers team and produced by Tsuruoka Fabric Industry Cooperative.
PHOTOGRAPHER: SUE MCNAB

BELOW: Norwegian Rain, *Double Breasted Raincoat II* (Mixed Black, full length) 100% recycled polyester, 2011. PHOTOGRAPHER: MAGNE SANDNES/ GRANDPEOPLE

Norwegian Rain approaches the goal of sustainable design from a different waste reduction strategy. The company uses two woven fabrics for the exterior of their garments, both manufactured in Japan, which are 100 per cent recycled polyester from plastic bottles. The high-performance material is both water-repellent and breathable, and took two years of hunting and testing to select. Alexander Helle, the company's founder, explains that his challenge is similar to that voiced by Dashing Tweeds: 'It is hard to find high-tech fabrics that are also eco-friendly and don't look technical. We are always trying to push the mindset of eco options that also push the direction of our aesthetic.'[19] A carbon offset fee is paid by the business to counter the transport of fabric woven in Japan to Europe, where the garments are produced, and in many cases back to Japan for sale, where their garments enjoy a loyal following.

Helle was torn between an education in design or business when he decided he 'wanted to know how to live' from his creative skills. When business studies led him to Milan, he found himself 'pulled back into the creative mindset'. Crucially, coming from Bergen – the rainiest city in Europe – his time in Milan was also the 'first time I was dry for more than two days, which was kind of pleasant'. The market's offering of rainwear showed him a real gap and Helle returned to Norway with the ambition to create 'hard-core rain gear that doesn't look or feel like rainwear'. Working with a bespoke tailor, T. Michael,

Norwegian Rain, *Single Breasted Raincoat* (Olive Green Herringbone, full length), 2011. 88% recycled polyester and 12% organic cotton, Dobby loom.

Norwegian Rain, *Double Breasted Raincoat I (Brown Herringbone, mid length)*, 2010. 88% recycled polyester and 12% organic cotton, Dobby loom.

PHOTOGRAPHER: MAGNE SANDNES/ GRANDPEOPLE

in Bergen, the company was launched. The sophisticated aesthetic and high technical specifications of their garments set them apart and offer durability, performance and style in a market saturated by fast fashion.

Moroccan designer **Soukaina Aziz El Idrissi**'s 'Poly-bond' project focuses on new uses for plastic waste. Harvesting materials from a newly established recycling plant near her family's home in Morocco, Aziz El Idrissi began to explore how continuous filament and plastic tape could find a new life in her weaving. Recycling is not yet an established solution to waste in Morocco, and the plant had collected a range of materials that for various reasons they were not yet able to process. 'I do feel that being Moroccan, it is important for me to do something that would somehow, someday, somewhere, help the environment that I grew up in by resourcing materials from there.'[20] For reasons of efficiency, Aziz El Idrissi searched the plant for materials 'that were already linear' and would readily translate into the weft. Elsewhere, she constructed the weft. Flakes from detergent bags made out of polypropylene, for example, were heat-pressed into flexible surfaces and reinforced using Bondaweb before being cut into fine strips and woven as weft on a monofilament and cellophane warp. The cellophane provides an eye-catching shimmer under light, while the monofilament proved 'sturdy', an important factor in creating textiles that would be strong enough to withstand a long second life.

Soukaina Aziz El Idrissi, *Junk Jacquard* (detail), from the 'Poly-bond' series, 2010. Monofilament and recycled polypropylene ribbon weft on a polyester warp, Jacquard weave. PHOTOGRAPHER: SOUKAINA AZIZ EL IDRISSI

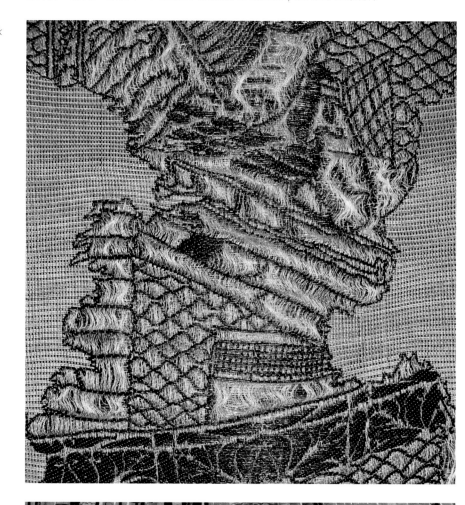

Soukaina Aziz El Idrissi, *Leno* (detail), from the 'Poly-bond' series, 2010. Hand-woven with weft of recycled plastic bags and warp of polyester, leno weave structure, laminated, eight-shaft hand loom. PHOTOGRAPHER: SOUKAINA AZIZ EL IDRISSI

When her research continued in London, where she graduated from the BA weaving course in Textile Design at Central Saint Martin's College of Art and Design in 2010, Aziz El Idrissi faced the questionable logic of shipping Moroccan plastic waste to England and switched her sources to plastic bags from H&M, Tesco and Zara. Her chosen materials may be ubiquitous, but they also bring with them their own restrictions: 'I have to work with the colours I am provided with. I couldn't dye the material because of needing extremely high temperatures to get the tint to set in and stay, so the colour palette is given by the materials. Instead, I create different combinations so that it does not look like it is made from plastic bags.' As well as materials, design imagery for her work comes from junkyards. 'I looked at the recycling plant as visual inspiration – stacks of plastic bottles condensed together provided the texture and shape.' Weaving, for all its technical challenges, remains her primary design focus. 'The material has to be woven; there is nothing you cannot weave with', Aziz El Idrissi proclaims. 'I don't see myself not weaving. Weaving satisfies my needs. I use it as a research tool as much as a design tool, because it allows me to understand the materials I am using so much more.'

The 'Salvage' series by American textile designer **Suzanne Tick** is hand-woven from dry-cleaning packaging. 'I grew up in a family where you saved things like metal cans and paper', Tick explains of her childhood in America's Midwest, where her father owned a third-generation recycling scrap metal facility.[21] Weaving with recycled wire offered Tick a personal way to honour her father's work. 'Metal for me represented my father and the years he worked at the salvage yard – the eldest son in the family had to take over the junkyard. There were other things he would have preferred to do with his life; he dutifully took over the company … I wanted to do something in memory of his work.'

Since 1981, Tick has been based in New York City as a commercial textile designer. With her studio located on a floor of her home, she is 'always trying to weave with what comes into the house, often to generate ideas for commercial work'. The packaging of her family's dry-cleaning proved to be an unexpectedly rich source of weft material. The three straight bars that make up each metal hanger, the metal hook at the top, the white cardboard tube that lines each hanger to prevent creases, and the metres of clear plastic shrouding each garment to preserve the cleaning have all made their way into the 'Salvage' series. When Tick first started to save the metal hangers in 2009, her intention was to cut a small amount of wire for use in a holiday card project for her commercial clients. She soon received an unanticipated call: what was the cost per yard for the material? The unusual commission, entitled *Refuse DC*, uses the bars of metal hangers to create a hand-woven textile that is 2.4 m (8 ft) tall and 3.9 m (12 ft 9 in.) wide. Commissioned for the Bill and Melinda Gates Foundation in Seattle,

Suzanne Tick, *Counterbalance*, 2011. Weft of 2,555 recycled wires from dry-cleaning hangers and sheath core fibre warp, hand-woven plain weave on 24-harness AVL loom.

PHOTOGRAPHER: SUZANNE TICK

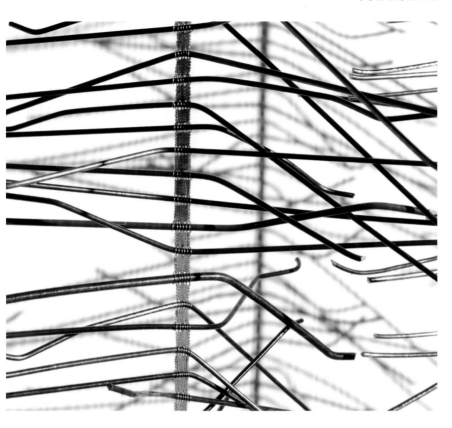

Suzanne Tick,
Counterbalance (detail).
PHOTOGRAPHER: SUZANNE TICK

Washington, by the architectural firm NBBJ, the materials were gathered from donations of dry-cleaning hangers made by the architectural firm's staff and shipped to Tick's studio weekly. Word got out, and soon Tick was receiving hangers not only from the architecture firm, but also from employees of the foundation and the contractor for the foundation's building construction, along with Tick's friends within the industry who had heard about the project. *Refuse DC* is now a wall of donated material that exists, to a large part, because of community enthusiasm and support for the project.

Much of Tick's commercial work is for KnollTextiles, where from 1997 to 2005 she was creative director and instrumental in the company's development of textiles that make use of post-consumer fibres. 'Clients want to know what ignites the inspiration behind each idea', she explains of the impact that the 'Salvage' series has had on her work as a commercial designer. 'Telling and tying in the whole design story is really important. By showing the woven structures of the art pieces, I can present the whole idea.' Like Aziz El Idrissi, Tick also sees her work with recycled materials as creating a loop of design references. The artwork that begins her commercial projects is often inspired by photographs and scans of her experiments with recycling. Finally, 'Salvage' is also about making human connections. 'The other nice thing is the sense

Suzanne Tick, *Hooked Up*, 2011. Weft of 5,040 recycled dry-cleaning hanger hooks on sheath core fibre warp, hand-woven tapestry weave on 24-harness AVL loom.

PHOTOGRAPHER: SUZANNE TICK

Suzanne Tick, *Refuse DC*, 2011. Weft of 3,470 wire coat hangers recycled from dry-cleaning packaging on sheath core fibre warp, hand-woven plain weave on 24-harness AVL loom.

PHOTOGRAPHER: SUZANNE TICK

of community', Tick comments about the somewhat unplanned impact of the series. For an upcoming show at the architecture, design, planning and consulting firm Gensler, Tick indicates that she 'will be teaching weaving classes in their offices for three months, one night a week. It is their responsibility to collect the materials they want to weave'. The recycling of the commonplace has started a cycle that is not only productive for Tick's design business, but is also connecting to a far broader community of enthusiasts.

Based in Berlin, the American artist **Travis Meinolf** encourages collaborative weaving. 'I think woven cloth is the ultimate example of human productivity', he declares of his commitment to the process.[22] Collaborative, community-based weaving is not as easy to set up as its textile counterparts of knitting or embroidery – techniques that use tools easily adapted for transportation. Meinolf concedes that it was 'hard work creating a transportable loom that was simple to set up and able to communicate the technique with [the] least frustration'. But with some necessary adaptations (including wheels) to his counterbalance floor loom, he now teaches workshops on it, as well as on small backstrap looms, in a surprising variety of locations: fields, bridges, even train stations have all provided sites for weaving.

For Meinolf, weaving is a group activity guided by a tool. 'Knitting, crochet and embroidery are more skill based; weaving is more tool based', he points out. 'Once you are taught how to operate a loom, it all revolves around the application of materials to the loom. It is directed by [the] tool.' Some may beg to differ that it is the tool that determines the weaving, particularly designers and artists known to challenge the technical parameters of woven production. But

LEFT: Travis Meinolf, *Folklore: Old New Forms*, 2011. Wool/synthetic weft and cotton warp, plain weave, two-harness counter-balance loom, Kunsthall Moen 44, Denmark.

PHOTOGRAPHER: IRIS MEINOLF

RIGHT: Travis Meinolf, *The Weaving Place* (detail), 2008–9. Wool weft and cotton warp, plain weave, rigid heddle looms, the Vancouver Art Gallery, Canada.

PHOTOGRAPHER: DORA VARGA LENCSES

LEFT: Travis Meinolf, *Folklore: Old New Forms*, 2011. Wool/synthetic weft and cotton warp, plain weave, two-harness counter-balance loom, Kunsthall Moen 44, Denmark.
PHOTOGRAPHER: IRIS MEINOLF

RIGHT: Travis Meinolf, wool weft and warp, counter-balance loom on wheels, Berlin, Germany, 2010.
PHOTOGRAPHER: IRIS MEINOLF

Meinolf works with community groups who are often experiencing weaving for the first time. At this introductory level, when the woven structure is new, the tools of weaving guide production in a way that a sewing needle or crochet hook does not. 'It is the detail and tedium of weaving that people will initially reject. It is actually a threshold, getting people to attempt to weave', he has observed. That said, he has also noticed that: 'Most who try [to hand-weave], will get entranced.'

One of Meinolf's motivations, during his workshops, is to 'get people to think about labour issues' and he sees some of the challenges of weaving as a good starting point for these important conversations. In stark contrast to typical patterns of individual consumption, the textiles created during his workshops often continue life as objects shared by the community. The 'invested community' (those who wove the work) decide what will happen to the weaving upon completion, and the setting of the workshop often has an impact on the outcome determined by the group. 'The highest contrast in context is institution based', he explains, compared to 'less formal gatherings'. '[The] more institutional the space [of the workshop], the more people try [to] make more formal decisions about the making process and afterlife. They work in "official mode", for example by

126

suggesting voting. This can be a strength, but seeing outcomes determined by [organic] groups is also interesting to watch.' Some groups decide to time-share the blankets they have woven and 'use the textile in shifts, passing it round the community so it is still used as a private object'. In large group projects, the textile is often donated to a local charity for use as a blanket. Still others decide to give away what has been made to people they meet by chance on the street.

Meinolf often finds that after his initial introduction, the group engages with the workshop information in their own language. 'When the group takes over and has a conversation in their own language then I'm more removed, which I find ideal', he remarks. Ultimately, the loom acts as a conversation point that helps to pull together disparate knowledge groups. Regardless of the setting: 'People generally make the same kinds of connections. People with previous experience or a heritage linked to textiles love sharing stories, and weaving is a tool for communication of other aspects of where people are coming from.'

In the winter of 2008, the American artist **Anne Wilson** produced *Wind-Up: Walking the Warp* at the Rhona Hoffman Gallery in Chicago. Over the course of six days, Wilson and nine assistants wound 36 m (118 ft) of warp on a giant frame set on the gallery floor. Dressed in white, the team walked, wound, meditated, ate and discussed the intentions and the meaning of their labour. From the snowy street outside, passers-by could observe the steady accumulation of a fluorescent warp. Production usually kept behind factory doors became a public performance. 'Understanding the complexities of production, Wilson demands that research and discussion become central components of the object itself', observes Chris Molinski of the artist's working strategy.[23] Reflecting on the project, Wilson volunteers, 'One important goal of the … performance was

Anne Wilson, *Wind-Up: Walking the Warp*, 2008. Performance and sculpture. First performed at the Rhona Hoffman Gallery, Chicago, 20–25 January 2008. Participants included Carla Duarte, Annie Egleson, Surabhi Ghosh, Jongock Kim, Rosemary Lee, Christy Matson, Rachel Moore, Jeroen Nelemans, Sara Rabinowitz, Rana Siegel, Mike Slattery and Anne Wilson.

PHOTOGRAPHER: SURABHI GHOSH

IMAGE COURTESY OF THE ARTIST AND RHONA HOFFMAN GALLERY, CHICAGO

Anne Wilson, *Wind-Up: Walking the Warp*, 2008. Performance and sculpture. First performed at the Rhona Hoffman Gallery, Chicago, USA.

to think through effective communication and the quality of a group process. We developed a collaborative team and a working method that allowed us to undertake the challenges of our particular production, both technical and social – we were working from the inside of a process and through our physical participation to understand time, labor, and cultural production.'[24]

Communal production continued in *Local Industry*, held two years later at the Knoxville Museum of Art in Tennessee. This time, 2,100 community volunteers, 79 weavers and numerous studio assistants contributed to a community weaving project.[25] An 'archive of production' listing all the contributors to the project, alphabetised by first names, runs to 11 pages.[26] The Knoxville Museum's surrounding area once enjoyed a thriving industrial textile industry, as well as a cottage industry of hand-weaving that provided much-needed economic sustenance for the region.[27] 'Local Industry' acted as a site-specific installation that invited every museum visitor to contribute to a collective weaving by winding a bobbin of thread on a hand-cranked bobbin

Weavers Tommy Scanlin and Gerry Forker finishing *Local Industry Cloth*, 2010, at the Knoxville Museum of Art, USA. PHOTOGRAPHER: KNOXVILLE MUSEUM OF ART

right and below:
Anne Wilson, *Local Industry Cloth* (details), 2010. Weft of donated mill fibre and cotton warp, weft-face plain weave hand-woven on floor loom.

PHOTOGRAPHER: JONATHAN BAGBY

COLLECTION KNOXVILLE MUSEUM OF ART

winder. Working with the community-wound bobbins, 'over three months, 79 experienced weavers produced visual sections of stripes in any combination'.[28] The resulting cloth measures 24 m (78 ft 9 in.) and '[It] remains in the museum's collection, a product for which there was no monetary exchange. The weft threads used in the "Local Industry" production were donated from the mills and textile factories (often from businesses facing closure). The work of each bobbin winder and each weaver was donated, and the museum charged no costs for admissions.'[29]

Jenni Sorkin observes, 'Consciously or not, the project has a utopian imperative, seeking to fill the void left when the Knoxville area lost a great deal of its textile manufacturing in the late 1980s. In 1988, a major apparel manufacturer closed its plant in nearby Blount County, where women were the majority workforce. Ostensibly, women make up the majority of Wilson's workforce as well, a faux cottage industry that mirrors social networking practices. Offering a democratized space for exchange and community, she makes visible the displacement (and, some would say, demotion) of textiles and its largely female workforce from American industry to the realm of cultural experience.'[30] Community is very much at the heart of Wilson's practice. These groups range from the modest and intimate – the volunteers who work intensively beside her to realise a project – to the local communities invested in the exhibition site, and finally the global network of labour and consumption linked to textiles. Reflecting on these recent works, Wilson explains the importance of developing 'a conceptual structure that involved a constellation of participants, leaders, sites, and audiences, and to actualize the use-function of the performed warp by weaving it into cloth'. 'This conceptual structure of art production can be likened to the woven textile itself – a cloth is created through the ordering of many individual parts and actions; the term "weaving" is historically used as a metaphor for ideas about coming together, for community.'[31]

Gabriel Dawe, *Plexus 4*, 2010. Polyester thread installation, 3.35 x 7.26 x 7.62 m (11 x 24 x 25 ft), installed Dallas Contemporary, USA.

PHOTOGRAPHER: KEVIN TODORA

Notes

Introduction

1. Anni Albers, *Anni Albers: On Designing* (Connecticut: Wesleyan University Press, 1943), pp.12–13.
2. Arthur Danto, *Sheila Hicks: Weaving as Metaphor* (New Haven and London: Yale University Press, 2006), p.33.
3. Ibid.

CHAPTER ONE Threads

1. Gabriel Dawe's quotes are from author's interview 5 July 2011.
2. Douglas Murphy, *Icon Magazine*, November 2010, p.48.
3. *Gravity's Loom* press release by the Indianapolis Museum of Art.
4. Gaston Nogues and Benjamin Ball 'Insta-llator 1 with the Variable Information Atomising Module', unpublished statement.
5. Ibid.
6. Benjamin Ball's quotes, unless otherwise stated, from author's interview 7 July 2011.
7. Susie MacMurray's quotes are from author's interview 26 May 2011.
8. Laura Thomas's quotes are from author's interview 22 June 2011.
9. Sue Lawty's quotes are from author's interview 1 August 2011.
10. Louise Glück, 'Disruption, Hesitation, Silence', *Proofs & Theories: Essays on Poetry* (New York: Ecco, 1994) pp.74–75.
11. Lauren Moriarty's quotes are from author's interview 28 July 2011.
12. Elana Herzog, 'Elana Herzog on Plaid' in New York Foundation for the Arts newsletter, 2007.
13. Regine Basha, 'Interview with Elana Herzog' in *Elana Herzog: Dewarped & Unweft* (Sedalia, Missouri: Daum Museum, 2010).
14. Op. cit.

CHAPTER TWO Light

1. Tamar Frank's quotes are from author's interview 7 July 2011.
2. Marianne Kemp's quotes are from author's interview 8 August 2011.

3. Kirsty McDougall's quotes, unless otherwise stated, are from author's interview 7 July 2011.

4. Kirsty McDougall, unpublished research statement.

5. Kirsty McDougall, 'A Case Study for Innovation in Contemporary Tweed', unpublished conference abstract, 2011.

6. Hiroko Takeda's statement accessed 10 August 2011 via http://www.hirokotakeda.com/about.php.

7. Hiroko Takeda's quotes, unless otherwise stated, are from author's interview 28 May 2011.

8. Op. cit.

9. Hiroko Takeda, e-mail correspondence 18 August 2011.

10. Christine Keller's quotes, unless otherwise stated, are from author's interview 7 July 2011.

11. Christine Keller e-mail 7 July 2011.

12. Ibid.

13. Hilde Hauan Johnsen's statement accessed via www.hildehauanjohnsen.no on 29 August 2011.

14. Ibid.

15. Ibid.

16. Hilde Hauan Johnsen's quotes, unless otherwise stated, are from author's interview 23 August 2011.

17. Op. cit.

18. Sarah Taylor e-mail correspondence 27 August 2011.

19. Sarah Taylor, *Art Textiles of the World: Great Britain* volume 3 (Brighton: Telos Art Publishing, 2006), p.46.

20. Sarah Taylor interview with author 2 September 2011.

21. Ibid.

22. Astrid Krogh quoted in Bradley Quinn, *Astrid Krogh: Light Tapestries* (Galerie Maria Wettergren catalogue, 2011).

23. Astrid Krogh's quotes, unless otherwise stated, are from author's interview 1 August 2011.

24. Priti Veja's quotes are from author's interview 5 August 2011.

25. Salt design statement accessed 7 August 2011 via http://www.salt-uk.com.

26. June Swindell, author's interview 9 June 2011.

27. June Swindell's quotes, unless otherwise stated, are from author's article first published in *Textile: Modern Carpets and Textiles* magazine in 2006.

28. Interview with Ainsley Hillard 7 July 2011.

29. Ainsley Hillard e-mail 15 August 2011.

30. Angela Maddock, *Ainsley Hillard: Traces* (Mission Gallery catalogue).

31. Op. cit.

CHAPTER THREE **Motion**

1. Philip Beesley accessed via http://www.hylozoicground.com/intro/intro03.html on 23 August 2011.

2. Fundacion Telefonica Jury statement accessed via http://www.hylozoicground.com/project/index.html on 23 August 2011.

3. Philip Beesley e-mail correspondence 8 April 2011.

4. Philip Beesley's quotes, unless otherwise stated, are from author's interview 6 May 2011.

5. Maria Blaisse's quotes are from author's interview 22 August 2011.

6. Barbara Layne's quotes are from author's interview 11 August 2011.

7. Zane Berzina's quotes, unless otherwise stated, are from author's interview 31 May 2011.

8. Zane Berzina e-mail correspondence 22 August 2011.

9. Ibid.

10. Maggie Orth's quotes, unless otherwise stated, are from author's interview 8 July 2011.

11. Maggie Orth accessed via http://www.maggieorth.com/art_100EAYears.html on 31 August 2011.

12. Elaine Ng Yan Ling's quotes are from author's interview 7 May 2011.

13. Edgar Alan Poe, 'A Descent Into the Maelstrom' accessed via http://www.pinkmonkey.com/dl/library1/desce_.pdf on 21 August 2011.

14. Lucy McMullen e-mail correspondence 22 August 2011.

15. Lucy McMullen's quotes, unless otherwise stated, are from author's interview 21 August 2011.

16. Philippa Brock's quotes, unless otherwise stated, are from author's interview 13 May 2011.

17. Philippa Brock, unpublished statement.

18. Philippa Brock, author's interview 28 August 2011.

19. Grethe Sørensen, 'From Traditional to Digital Tools', *Textile Society of America Proceedings 2010*, University of Nebraska-Lincoln, accessed 26 July 2011 via http://digitalcommons.unl.edu/tsaconf/51/.

20. Ibid.

21. Ibid.

22. Grethe Sørensen's quotes, unless otherwise stated, are from author's interview 26 July 2011.

23. Op. cit.

24. Op. cit.

25. Op. cit.

CHAPTER FOUR Sound

1. Christy Matson's quotes, unless otherwise stated, are from author's interview 16 May 2011.
2. Matson's quotes about Portland residency are from author's interview 28 July 2011.
3. Lars Preisser's quotes from statement accessed via http://larspreissertextiles. blogspot.com on 22 August 2011.
4. Dr Gro Frølund, 'Lullaloom 2005–2007', unpublished essay.
5. Lise Frølund statement from *Thinking Different: Thinking JacquART* (Haslach an der Muhl, Austria: Textile Kultur Haslach, 2009).
6. Ibid.
7. Lise Frølund's quotes, unless otherwise stated, are from author's interview 22 August 2011.
8. Lise Frølund e-mail correspondence 22 August 2011.
9. Elin Igland's quotes are from author's interview 19 August 2011.
10. Elin Igland e-mail correspondence 31 August 2011.
11. For sound recording of Sonic Fabric, see http://www.sonicfabric.com/ sound_video.html.
12. Sonic Fabric statement accessed via http://www.sonicfabric.com/about. html on 27 August 2011.
13. Alyce Santoro's quotes, unless otherwise stated, are from author's interview 28 May 2011.
14. Alyce Santoro e-mail correspondence 11 August 2011.
15. Sonic Fabric statement accessed via http://www.sonicfabric.com/about. html on 27 August 2011.
16. Drahomira Hampl's quotes are from e-mail correspondence 11 August 2011, translated by Katrin Berndt.
17. Nadia-Anne Ricketts's quotes are from author's interview 15 May 2011.
18. Eleanor Pritchard's quotes are from author's interview 5 August 2011.
19. Aleksandra Gaca statement in *Thinking Different: Thinking JacquART* (Haslach an der Mühl, Austria: Textile Kultur Haslach, 2009).
20. Ibid.
21. Aleksandra Gaca's quotes, unless otherwise stated, are from author's interview 21 August 2011.
22. Aleksandra Gaca e-mail correspondence 24 August 2011.
23. Ismini Samanidou's and Gary Allson's quotes are from author's interview 7 July 2011.

CHAPTER FIVE Emotion

1. See Louise Bourgeois, 'A Memoir' in *Louise Bourgeois: The Fabric Works*, edited by Germano Celant (Milan: Skira, 2010), pp.29–34.

2. See, for example, Louise Bourgeois with Lawrence Rinder, *Louise Bourgeois: Drawings and Observations* (London: Bullfinch Press, 1995).

3. Rozsika Parker, 'Introduction', *The Subversive Stitch* (reprinted 2010 by I.B. Tauris Co. Ltd., first published by The Women's Press Ltd., 1984), p. xviii–xix.

4. Ane Henriksen, *Lady Sings the Blues* (Kunstindustrimuseet 2011 exhibition catalogue). Quote first printed in *Art Textiles of the World: Scandinavia* (Brighton: Telos, 2004), p.48.

5. Ibid.

6. Jette Hartvig, 'A Closed Chapter' in *Lady Sings the Blues* (Kunstindustrimuseet 2011 exhibition catalogue), p.55.

7. Louise Mazanti, 'Our Body – the World's Body' in *Lady Sings the Blues* (Kunstindustrimuseet 2011 exhibition catalogue), p.23.

8. Ibid, p.48.

9. Shane Waltener quotes from e-mail correspondence 2 August 2011.

10. Elizabeth Wayland Barber, *Women's Work: The First 20,000 Years, Women, Cloth and Society in Early Times* (London: W. W. Norton & Co., 1994), pp.153–54.

11. Kathryn Sullivan Kruger, 'Clues and Cloth: Seeking Ourselves in "The Fabric of Myth"' in *The Fabric of Myth*, exhibition catalogue (Warwickshire: Compton Verney, 2008), p.18.

12. Jeroen Vinken's quotes, unless otherwise stated, are from author's interview 25 May 2011.

13. Jeroen Vinken e-mail correspondence 4 August 2011.

14. Jeroen Vinken e-mail correspondence 15 August 2011.

15. Brigitte de Swart, *Jeroen Vinken* (Amsterdam: Beeldrecht), p.21.

16. Op. cit.

17. Jeroen Vinken e-mail correspondence 8 August 2011.

18. Liz Williamson's quotes, unless otherwise stated, are from author's interview 28 August 2011.

19. Gary Sangster, *Liz Williamson: Textiles* (exhibition catalogue). Published to coincide with the exhibition Liz Williamson: Textiles, part of the 'Living Treasures: Masters of Australian Craft' series 8 November 2008–11 January 2009 at Object Gallery, Sydney.

20. Lucy Brown e-mail correspondence 20 August 2011.

21. Ibid.

22. Lucy Brown, unpublished working artist's statement.

23. Lucy Brown's quotes, unless otherwise stated, are from author's interview 20 August 2011.

24. Catherine Harper, *Thread Bare* (exhibition catalogue), exhibition at Rochester Art Gallery, England, 13 February–25 April 2010.

25. Lucy Brown, unpublished working artist's statement.
26. Glenn Adamson, 'A Twist in the Tale' in *Anne Wilson: Wind/Rewind/Weave* (Knoxville: Knoxville Museum of Art and Whitewalls, 2011) p.15.
27. Lia Cook's quotes are from author's interview 5 August 2011.

CHAPTER SIX Community

1. Petter Hellsing's quotes, unless otherwise stated, are from author's interview 6 July 2011.
2. Petter Hellsing e-mail correspondence 22 August 2011.
3. Runa Carlsen's quotes, unless otherwise stated, are from author's interview 27 July 2011.
4. Runa Carlsen e-mail correspondence 16 August 2011.
5. Ibid.
6. Transport for London press release, 'New Tube Seating Fabric Captures the Spirit of London', 9 July 2010.
7. Emma Sewell's quotes are from author's interview 7 July 2011.
8. Ptolemy Mann accessed via www.ptolemymann.com/colour_statement.php on 21 August 2011.
9. Ibid.
10. Ptolemy Mann's quotes, unless otherwise stated, are from author's interview 5 July 2011.
11. Rosita Missoni's quotes are from e-mail correspondence 1 September 2011.
12. *ao for Gainsborough* interior fabric collection press release.
13. Ibid.
14. *KIRAKIRA* published by Nuno Corporation, 1999, p.45.
15. *SUKÉSUKÉ* published by Nuno Corporation, 1997, p.47.
16. *BOROBORO* published by Nuno Corporation, 1997, p.45.
17. NUNO e-mail correspondence with author 25 August 2011.
18. See http://exhibitions.cooperhewitt.org/Why-Design-Now/project/kibiso-bookshelf-futsu-crisscross-and-suzushi-stripe-textiles, accessed 29 August 2011.
19. Alexander Helle's quotes from author's interview 25 May 2011.
20. Soukaina Aziz El Idrissi's quotes from author's interview 26 July 2011.
21. Suzanne Tick's quotes are from author's interview 7 August 2011.
22. Travis Meinolf's quotes are from author's interview 27 May 2011.
23. Chris Molinski, 'Notes on the Exhibition' in *Anne Wilson: Wind/Rewind/Weave* (Knoxville: Knoxville Museum of Art and Whitewalls, 2011) p.3.
24. Anne Wilson, 'Notes on Wind-Up: Walking the Warp' in *Anne Wilson: Wind/Rewind/Weave* (Knoxville: Knoxville Museum of Art and Whitewalls, 2011) p.44.

25. Op. cit. p.1.

26. See *Anne Wilson: Wind/Rewind/Weave* (Knoxville: Knoxville Museum of Art and Whitewalls, 2011) pp.108–119.

27. Philis Alvic, 'The Story of a Tennessee Weaver' in *Anne Wilson: Wind/Rewind/Weave* (Knoxville: Knoxville Museum of Art and Whitewalls, 2011) p.61.

28. Molinski, p.4.

29. Ibid.

30. Jenni Sorkin, 'Constructing Community' in *Anne Wilson: Wind/Rewind/Weave* (Knoxville: Knoxville Museum of Art and Whitewalls, 2011) pp.35–36.

31. Anne Wilson in *Anne Wilson: Wind/Rewind/Weave* (Knoxville: Knoxville Museum of Art and Whitewalls, 2011) p.95.

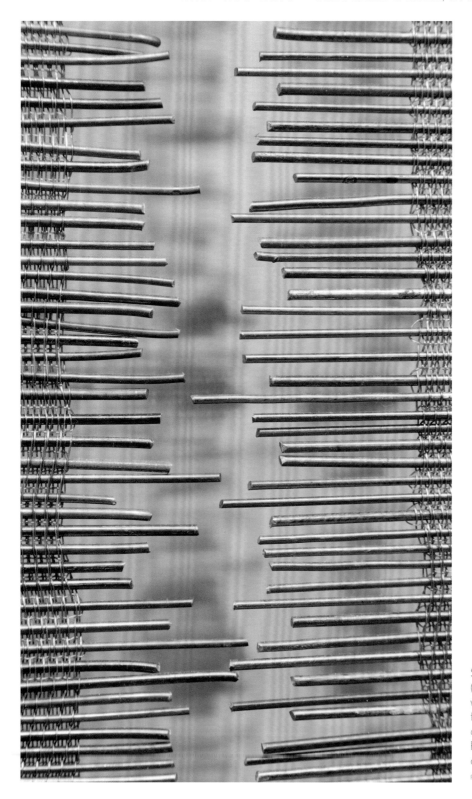

Suzanne Tick, *Refuse DC* (detail), 2011. Weft of 3,470 wire coat hangers recycled from dry-cleaning packaging on sheath core-fibre warp, hand-woven plain weave on 24-harness AVL loom.

PHOTOGRAPHER: SUZANNE TICK

Further Reading

Anni Albers, *Selected Writings on Design* (Middletown: Wesleyan University Press, 2000, first published 1965).

Elissa Auther, *String, Felt, Thread: The Hierarchy of Art and Craft in American Art* (London: University of Minnesota Press, 2010).

Ingrid Bachmann and Ruth Scheuing (eds), *Material Matters: the Art and Culture of Contemporary Textiles* (Toronto: YYZ Books, 2002).

Pennina Barnett, 'Rugs R Us (And Them)', *Third Text* (no. 30, spring 1995), pp.13–28.

Roland Barthes, *The Pleasure of the Text*, trans. Richard Miller (New York: Hill & Wang: 1975), p.64.

Susan S. Bean, 'Gandhi and Khadi, the Fabric of Indian Independence' in *Cloth and Human Experience*, Annette B. Weiner and Jane Schneider (eds) (London: Smithsonian Institution Press, 1989), pp.355–76.

Italo Calvino, *Invisible Cities* (London: Vintage Books, 1997), pp.67–8.

Mildred Constantine and Laurel Reuter, *Whole Cloth* (New York: The Monacelli Press, 1997).

Janis Jefferies, *Selvedges: Writings and Artworks Since 1980*, (Norwich: Norwich Gallery, 2000).

Mamle Kabu, 'The End of Skill' in *Dreams, Miracles and Jazz*, H. Habile and K. Sesay (eds) (Johannesburg: Picador Africa, 2008) pp. 14-29.

Sylvie Krüger, *Textile Architecture* (Berlin: Jovis Verlag, 2009).

Joan Livingstone and John Ploof (eds), *The Object of Labor: Art, Cloth, and Cultural Production* (Chicago: School of Art Institute of Chicago Press; Cambridge and London: The MIT Press, 2007).

Sadie Plant, *Zeroes and Ones: Digital Women and the New Technoculture* (London: Doubleday, 1997).

Ruth Scheuing, 'Penelope and the Unraveling of History' in *New Feminist Art Criticism*, Katy Deepwell (ed.) (Manchester: Manchester University Press, 1995) pp.188–95.

Peter Stallybrass, 'Marx's Coat' in *Border Fetishisms: Material Objects in Unstable Places*, Patricia Spyer (ed.) (London: Routledge, 1998).

Kathryn Sullivan Kruger, *Weaving the Word: The Metaphorics of Weaving and Female Textual Production* (London and Selinsgrove: Associated University Press and Susquehanna University Press, 2001).

Elizabeth Wayland Barber, *Women's Work: The First 20,000 Years: Women, Cloth and Society in Early Times* (London: W.W. Norton & Company, 1994) pp.232–56.

Catherine M. Zegher (ed.). *The Precarious: The Art and Poetry of Cecilia Vicuña* (London: University Press of New England, 1997).

Susie MacMurray, *Promenade*, 2010. Cotton thread installation, Kedleston Hall, Derby, England.

PHOTOGRAPHER: SUSIE MACMURRAY

Index

Allson, Gary 86–7
Antoni, Janine 100–1
ao for Gainsborough 114–15
Aziz El Idrissi, Soukaina 119–21

Ball-Nogues Studio 14–16
Beesley, Philip 50–4
Berzina, Zane 58–60
Blaisse, Maria 54–5
Bourgeois, Louise 88–90
Brock, Philippa 65–7
Brown, Lucy 97–100

Carlsen, Runa 107–9
Cook, Lia 100, 102–3

D'Arcey, Emma 114–15
Dashing Tweeds 31–4
Dawe, Gabriel 10–14, 132

Frank, Tamar 28–9
Frølund, Lise 75–7

Gaca, Aleksandra 8, 84–6

Hampl, Drahomira 81–2
Hauan Johnsen, Hilde 38–9
Helle, Alexander 117–9
Hellsing, Petter 104–6
Henriksen, Ane 90–2
Herrick, Laurie 72

Herzog, Elana 24–7
Hillard, Ainsley 47–9
Hills, Guy 31–3
Hotel Missoni 114

Ingland, Elin 76, 78–9

Keller, Christine 36–8
Kemp, Marianne 30–1
KnollTextiles 123
Krogh, Astrid 6, 42–3

Lawty, Sue 20–2
Layne, Barbara 56–7

MacMurray, Susie 16–18, 142
Mann, Ptolemy 112–13
Matson, Christy 72–3
McDougall, Kirsty 31–3
McMullen, Lucy 63–5
Meinolf, Travis 125–7
Metasynth software 72
Missoni, Rosita 114
Moriarty, Lauren 22–4

Ng Yan Ling, Elaine 62–3
Norwegian Rain 117–9
NUNO 116–7

Orth, Maggie 60–1

Penelope myth 92, 94
performance 100–1, 127–31
Preissser, Lars 73–5
Pritchard, Eleanor 84

Raffnsøe, Hanne 75–7
recycled materials 81, 114–5, 117–9,
    121–5
Ricketts, Nadia-Anne 82–3

Salt 45–6
Salt 9
Samanidou, Ismini 86–7
Santoro, Alyce 80–1
Santoro, Jeannette 81
Scotweave software 86
Sørensen, Grethe 67–9
Spurgin, Karen 114–15

Sudo, Reiko 116
Swindell, June 45–6

Takeda, Hiroko 35
tapestry 88–92
Taylor, Sarah 8
Thomas, Laura 18–19
Tick, Suzanne 121–3, 140

Urstad, Maia 38–9

Veja, Priti 42–5
Vinken, Jeroen 94–7

Wallace & Sewell 109–11
Waltener, Shane 92–4
Williamson, Liz 97
Wilson, Anne 127–31